Grammar Talk

Grammar Talk

Anthony C. Winkler

Jo Ray McCuen
Glendale Community College

Pearson Education

PRENTICE HALL Upper Saddle River, New Jersey 07458

Library of Congress Cataloging-in-Publication Data

Winkler, Anthony C.
    Grammar talk/Anthony C. Winkler, Jo Ray McCuen.
      p. cm.
   Includes index.
   ISBN 0-13-628173-7 (paper)
   1. English language—Grammar—Problems, exercises, etc.
I. McCuen, Jo Ray, II. Title.
PE1112.W56   1997
428.2—dc21   97-7007
                             CIP

Editorial Director: Charlyce Jones Owen
Senior Acquisitions Editor: Maggie Barbieri
Editorial Assistant: Joan Polk
Developmental Editor: Harriett Prentiss
Director of Production and Manufacturing: Barbara Kittle
Managing Editor: Bonnie Biller
Project Manager: Karen Trost
Project Liaison: Shelly Kupperman
Manufacturing Manager: Nick Sklitsis
Prepress and Manufacturing Buyer: Mary Ann Gloriande
Creative Design Director: Leslie Osher
Art Director: Anne Bonanno Nieglos
Cover and Interior Designer: Carmela Pereira
Cover Art: Cover background image copyright © 1996 Photodisc, Inc.
Supervisor of Production Services: Lori Clinton
Marketing Manager: Rob Mejia

This book was set in 11/13 New Century Schoolbook by PH Formatting
and printed and bound by Courier Companies, Inc.
The cover was printed by The Lehigh Press, Inc.

© 1997 by Prentice-Hall, Inc.
Simon & Schuster/A Viacom Company
Upper Saddle River, NJ 07458

Printed in the United States of America

10   9   8   7   6   5   4   3   2

ISBN 0-13-628173-7

Prentice-Hall International (UK) Limited, *London*
Prentice-Hall of Australia Pty. Limited, *Sydney*
Prentice-Hall Canada Inc., *Toronto*
Prentice-Hall Hispanoamericana, S.A., *Mexico*
Prentice-Hall of India Private Limited, *New Delhi*
Prentice-Hall of Japan, Inc., *Tokyo*
Simon & Schuster Asian Pte. Ltd., *Singapore*
Editora Prentice-Hall do Brasil, Ltda., *Rio de Janeiro*

Contents

Preface

Grammar Talk takes as its starting point the assumption that grammar in the native speaker is a built-in skill, not an added-on one, and that the best sense for grammar in the native speaker is the ear. This is not a radical idea. In fact, it is almost self-evident. People speak the language they hear spoken around them from their days in the crib. An Englishman raised in a genteel drawing room will emerge from it speaking like an Englishman raised in a genteel drawing room. Transplant that same infant soul to an urban area like the New York Bronx, and he will grow up to speak like an urban soul raised in the New York Bronx. We have never seen an exception to this observation, and if one exists, it can only be the strongest possible argument for reincarnation. The plain fact is that we learn to speak our mother tongue not from a book, but from using our ears.

Yet, as English teachers, we know that many of our students neither speak nor write what we have been trained to call "good grammar." They use fragments; they punctuate badly; they misplace modifiers and garble sentences; they speak and write slang. How can we claim that a speaker's ear for grammar is so sensitive when all around us we have evidence to the contrary?

We can make this claim because these examples are not errors of bad grammar, but of inappropriate usage. If you are raised in a culture where *ain't* is widely accepted as an everyday verb, you will grow up to speak and write *ain't*. But since *ain't* is regarded today as nonstandard and unacceptable usage in formal writing, it is our job as English teachers to wean students off that word when the circumstances demand the formality of Standard English. However, to do so is not to demean *ain't* and those who use it. Some circumstances may indeed call for the use of *ain't*, but the classroom is not one of them.

Usage variations aside, it is still a fact that all native speakers have within them an ear for grammar that foreign speakers do not share; that is the prime assumption behind the pedagogy of *Grammar Talk*. We realize, however, that there are occasions when the ear is utterly at odds with the formal rule and of no help whatsoever in deciding what is right and appropriate. A case in point is the infamous *between you and I*. If we were to believe many politicians and a surprising array of other prominent men and women, we'd think this construction was right. Yet the formal rule declares *between you and me* to be the right form. A unique feature of *Grammar Talk* is the *Ear Alert* warnings provided in such instances. We first explain the formal rule; we then show how its practice in everyday speech varies from the rule. Finally, the *Ear Alert* label and distinctive icon in the margin warn students that this is a point of grammar on which the ear simply cannot be trusted.

Throughout *Grammar Talk,* our explanations of grammar rules

- emphasize functional problems, not descriptive grammar.
- use a minimum of terminology.
- give short, pointed explanations with a light touch.
- are followed by immediate practice.
- come with abundant exercises that include paragraphs for editing and sentences for reading aloud.
- are followed by a short summary of every main point (*In a Nutshell*).

Finally, every chapter ends with the following three types of exercises:

- A *Unit Test* that tests student mastery of the chapter.
- A *Unit Talking Assignment* that gives students the opportunity to interact in group sessions and put their ear to use in practicing the contents of the chapter.
- A *Unit Writing Assignment* that gives students the chance to apply the principles they have just learned.

Grammar, we know, usually strikes students as a grim business. To overcome this initial resistance, we have tried hard to make our explanations deft and light, to explain everything step by step and carefully, to drill immediately after explaining any rule or principle, and to respect and encourage the use of the student's innate "ear" for grammar.

Our thanks to Maggie Barbieri, the senior acquisitions editor at Prentice Hall, who encouraged our efforts every step of the way, and to the production and manufacturing staff at Prentice Hall: Bonnie Biller, Senior Managing Editor; Karen Trost, Project Manager; Lori Clinton, Formatting; Mary Ann Gloriande, Senior Buyer; Leslie Osher, Creative Design Director; and Anne Bonanno Nieglos, Art Director.

We would also like to thank the following reviewers: Stephanie Barnett, University of Maryland Eastern Shore; Lisa Berman, Miami Dade Community College; Diana M. Bach, Northeastern State Technical College; Karen Standridge, Pikes Peak Community College; Lois Hassan, Henry Ford Community College; Nancy Barlow, Brookhaven College; Jayne Williams, Texarkana College; Scott Kassner, Minneapolis Community College; Gary Zacharias, Palomar College.

In every enterprise of this kind, there lurks in the background one indispensable person who has had a significant and influential part in the outcome. Usually, this person is a freelance editor hired by the publisher to prod the writers into doing their utmost. In our case, the unsung hero who played this role was freelancer Harriett Prentiss. She goaded; she prodded; she corrected, edited, influenced, rewrote, and encouraged. She occasionally drove us mad; but she made us do more than our utmost. She made us do our best. Thanks, Harriett.

Anthony C. Winkler
Jo Ray McCuen

About the Authors

Anthony C. Winkler was born in Kingston, Jamaica, and educated at Mt. Alvernia Academy and Cornwall College in Montego Bay, Jamaica. In 1962, he came to the United States to attend school, and received an A.A. from Citrus College, and a B.A. and M.A. from California State University at Los Angeles.

For seven years, he taught as a part-time evening college instructor while working full time as a book representative first for Appleton Century Crofts, and then for Scott, Foresman.

Winkler began collaborating with Jo Ray McCuen in 1973, and became a full-time freelance writer in 1976. He is the author of numerous textbooks, trade books (including *Bob Marley: An Intimate Portrait by His Mother*), and screenplays (including *The Lunatic*, based on his second novel). He lives in Atlanta with his wife and two children.

Jo Ray McCuen was born in Belgium and grew up in Europe, coming to the United States for her college education. She received her B.A. from Pacific Union College and her M.A. and Ph.D. from the University of Southern California. While working on her doctorate, McCuen was hired to teach English at Glendale Community College, from which she retired in 1996.

A chance meeting in 1973 with Tony Winkler, who was a college textbook sales representative, led to a partnership that has produced fifteen coauthored textbooks used at colleges and universities across the country.

McCuen has one son, David Cotton, a perinatologist at Wayne State University. When not revising her textbooks and writing new ones, McCuen enjoys traveling, reading, opera, snow skiing, and tennis.

Grammar Talk

The Basic Sentence

> "Every sentence—no matter how long and complex—contains at its heart a kernel sentence."

A sentence is a group of words that expresses a complete thought. This completeness is what your speaker's ear uses to recognize a sentence. If someone said to you, "Leaf," you'd probably reply, "What?" ("What do you mean?") However, if someone said, "A leaf fell," you'd probably reply, "So what?" meaning that you understand but don't care. You responded differently because the second statement is complete enough for you to understand it.

Subject and Verb

To be complete, every sentence must have a subject and a verb. In its simplest form, the **subject** is someone who does something:

> John spoke.
>
> Mary ran.
>
> Jeannie laughed.

John, Mary, and Jeannie are the simple subjects of these sentences.

Naturally, the subject of a sentence can also be something rather than someone.

> The plane flew.
>
> The ship sailed.
>
> The house collapsed.
>
> Greed hurts.

The word that tells what the subject does or did is called the **verb**. From the examples above, we know that John *spoke*, Mary *ran*, and Jeannie *laughed*. We also know that the plane *flew*, the ship *sailed*, the house *collapsed*, and greed *hurts*.

Each of these examples is called a kernel sentence. A **kernel sentence** is the smallest sentence possible. Here are some other kernel sentences:

> Run!

Halt!

Go!

These kernel sentences are commands. The subject (you) is implied:

[You] run!

[You] halt!

[You] go!

Every sentence—no matter how long and complex—contains at its heart a kernel sentence. For example, consider this kernel sentence:

John spoke.

We can add words to it, making it longer and more detailed. Its heart, though, will still be the basic kernel sentence: John spoke. Here are some examples:

At noon before a crowd of students, *John spoke.*

John, in a red plaid coat and checkered pants, *spoke.*

Knowing the crowd was against him, *John spoke.*

John spoke at twelve o'clock in the blazing sun.

At twelve o'clock, *John spoke* in the blazing sun.

When we read a sentence, we know who did what or what happened and to whom. Without the subject and verb of the kernel sentence, for example, each of the phrases below is incomplete:

At noon before a crowd of students.	**(What happened?)**
In a red plaid coat and checkered pants.	**(What are you talking about? What did he or she do?)**
Knowing the crowd was against him.	**(Who? What happened?)**
At twelve o'clock in the blazing sun.	**(What happened?)**

To find the subject of a sentence, simply do this: Identify the verb. Then ask "Who?" or "What?" in front of it. The answer will be the subject. For example, in the sentence *John spoke*, we know the verb is *spoke*. If we ask "Who spoke?" the answer is the subject, John.

This simple test will also help you find the subject of a sentence worded as a question. Consider these examples:

When did John speak?

Did John speak at noon?

Why did John speak at noon?

If we ask, "Who?" before the verb *did speak*, the answer is the same: John, John, and John.

In a Nutshell

- A sentence always expresses a complete thought.

- A sentence always includes a subject and verb.

- A kernel sentence is the smallest sentence possible.

PRACTICING 1

In each of these sentences, underline the subject once and the verb twice. In questions, underline both verbs.

Example: The <u>bird</u> <u>chirped</u>.

1. The house burned.

2. The car sputters.

3. Jane Alexandra James laughed.

4. Why does Sally dance?

5. The thingamabob spins.

6. Computers crash.

7. How does money talk?

8. Horses neigh.

9. Kings ruled.

10. Elves exist.

PRACTICING 2

Underline the kernel sentence in each of these sentences.

Example: Clutching her red handbag, <u>the woman ran after the bus</u>.

1. Jane jumped into the pool.

2. Looking hard in the mirror, John smiled proudly.

3. Mary was happy to be at the party.

4. Jack Horner, a happy grin on his ugly face, ate.

5. Quite by accident, she bumped the chair.

6. The ship hit an iceberg.

7. We skied all day.

8. The trolls played under the bridge.

9. Whether he admits it or not, he often lies.

10. We know plenty about the case.

PRACTICING 3

Write *S* beside any construction you think is a sentence and *NS* if you think the construction is not one. If the construction is not a sentence, turn it into one in the space provided. Remember that a sentence must express a complete thought and contain a subject and verb.

1. _____ The green hat.

_____

2. _____ Mice squeak.

_____

3. _____ The black limousine with shiny tires.

_____

4. _____ The bat slept.

_____

5. _____ Sheila snored.

_____

6. _____ Running fast.

_____

7. _____ The ocean roared.

_____

8. _____ Setting the table.

_____

9. _____ Traffic jamming jokers.

_____

10. _____ Hear me, please!

Prepositional Phrases

Sometimes it's easy to spot the subject of a sentence, but sometimes it isn't. For example, what is the subject of this sentence?

> One of Mary's friends gave her a surprise party.

If we apply the test of asking "Who?" before *gave*, we find that *One* is the subject. Because the prepositional phrase *of Mary's friends* comes before the verb *gave,* you might mistake *Mary's friends* for the subject.

A **preposition** is a word that shows the relationship between two things; a **prepositional phrase** is a group of words beginning with a preposition. A preposition always has an **object**—usually a noun or pronoun that follows it. The preposition and its object make up the prepositional phrase. Here is an example:

> He put the book on the table.

Here the preposition is *on*, and the object is *table*. Remember this formula:

Preposition	+	Object	=	Prepositional phrase
on		the table		on the table
to		the sea		to the sea
of		the college		of the college
from		the store		from the store

Below is a list of the most common prepositions:

about	beside	like	under
above	besides	near	underneath
across	between	of	until
after	beyond	off	up
against	by	on	upon
along	despite	out	with
among	down	outside	within
around	during	over	without
at	except	past	throughout
before	for	since	through
behind	from	inside	
below	in	to	
beneath	into	toward	

One way to avoid mistaking a preposition for the subject of a sentence is to cross out all the prepositional phrases in any sentence whose subject you're trying to find. Here are some examples:

The driver ~~of the car~~ spoke to the officer.

The answers ~~to the test~~ were not given.

Every student ~~from our school~~ loves cold weather.

In a Nutshell

- A preposition is a word that shows the relationship between two things; a prepositional phrase is a preposition and its object.

- Don't mistake a word in a prepositional phrase for the subject of a sentence.

- If in doubt, cross out the prepositional phrase.

PRACTICING 4

For each of the following, create a prepositional phrase. Then write a complete sentence using the prepositional phrase.

1. above _____

_____

_____

2. through _____

_____

_____

3. inside _____

_____

_____

4. during _____

_____

_____

5. throughout _____

_____

_____

6. underneath _____

_____

_____

7. without _____

_____

_____

8. toward _____

_____

_____

9. around _____

_____

_____

10. in _____

_____

_____

PRACTICING 5

Exchange your answers to the Practicing 4 exercise with a class-mate. Underline the subject and verb in each of your partner's sentences. If you disagree about the subject and verb of any sentence, discuss it with other classmates.

PRACTICING 6

Cross out the prepositional phrase or phrases in each of the sentences below. Then identify the subject by circling it.

Example: The (box) is ~~on the top shelf in the closet~~.

1. He jumped the fence and ran across the field.

2. The son of David nodded.

3. After the singing, they went into the dining room for dinner.

4. I will be at the library until 4:00.

5. She is a woman of her word.

6. For your love, I give everything.

7. We sat near Louise, in the back row.

8. We sailed up the lazy river.

9. Put it on the shelf, behind the suitcase.

10. She backed out of the driveway without looking both ways.

Action Verbs and Linking Verbs

Verbs tell us who did what action in a sentence. What action, though, does *is* describe? In fact, it describes no action because *is* is a linking verb.

Indeed, there are two main kinds of verbs: action verbs and linking verbs. **Action verbs** describe an action. They tell us that the subject did a particular something. Here are examples:

Mary jumped off the chair.

Peter threw the ball.

Adam wrote an essay.

Each of these verbs describes a definite action: jumping, throwing, and writing. If someone asked you to mimic any of these actions, you could easily act out someone jumping, throwing, or writing. What if, however, someone asked you to mimic the action behind the verb *is*? You couldn't do it, because *is*, although a verb, describes no action and is instead a linking verb.

A **linking verb** connects the subject to other words that say something about it. Here are some examples:

Cathy is an accountant.

Harry looks tired.

Mary seems happy to be home.

The linking verb *is* connects the subject *Cathy* to the words *an accountant*, which is Cathy's job. Likewise, *Harry* is linked to *tired* by the linking verb *looks*, and *Mary* to *happy to be at home* by the linking verb *seems*. Linking verbs get their name because they link the subject to other words that tell us something about them. These other words are called **complements** because they "complete" the subject by renaming or describing it. So Cathy is *an accountant* (another name for Cathy), and Harry looks *tired* (describes his appearance).

Here are some other examples of complements:

The whole day was a <u>disaster</u>.

The mayor is his <u>mother.</u>

The milk smells <u>sour</u>.

Granny is the youngest <u>lawyer</u> in the firm.

Old bones become <u>brittle</u>.

Here is a list of some common linking verbs:

am	sound
are	look
has been	appear
is	seem
was	taste
were	smell

Don't mistake the complement of a sentence for its subject. Remember, to find the subject of a sentence, ask "Who?" or "What?" before the verb. The answer will be the subject. So, for example, in the sentence, *Granny is the youngest lawyer in the firm*, first identify the verb *is* and then ask "Who is?" The answer, Granny, is the subject.

PRACTICING 7

In the space provided, underline the verb and write *AV* beside sentences that contain an action verb or *LV* beside those that contain a linking verb.

1. _____ *Little Red Riding Hood* is a famous fairy tale.

2. _____ Those years seem so sad to me.

3. _____ The students shuffled into the auditorium.

4. _____ Jack tripped me on the football field.

5. _____ His father handed him the broom.

6. _____ The young minister looked awkward.

7. _____ All this was most upsetting.

8. _____ The colt nuzzled my hand.

9. _____ We explored the streams in the winter afternoons.

10. _____ The street was filled with potholes.

PRACTICING 8

In each of the following sentences, circle the linking verb and underline the complement.

Example: She (is) lovely.

1. They were careful.

2. Otto is a St. Bernard.

3. She was the team leader both years.

   4. Her smile looked phony.

   5. The judge's memory was not clear.

   6. Does the cheese smell bad?

   7. First graders often feel bewildered.

   8. The river looks murky.

   9. Jealousy is a hurtful emotion.

   10. Her purse is a suitcase.

Helping Verbs

Verbs sometimes need additional words, called **helping verbs**, to express the past, present, and future. In the five sentences below the complete verb is underlined:

The children <u>are eating</u> at noon.	**(present)**
The children <u>will eat</u> at noon.	**(future)**
The children <u>had eaten</u> before the storm arrived.	**(past)**
The children <u>were eating</u> when he knocked.	**(past)**

Here, for example, are some of the many forms of the verb *work*. Notice the many different helping verbs.

works	should have been working	will have worked
worked	can work	would have worked
is working	would have been working	has worked
was working	will be working	should have worked
may work	had been working	must have worked
should work	worked	having worked
will work	have worked	did work
does work	has worked	had worked

Occasionally, words that are not part of the complete verb will come between the helping verb and the main verb. Here are some examples, with the words underlined:

She has <u>already</u> left.

They could have <u>definitely</u> fallen.

All of us had <u>quickly</u> disappeared.

We will <u>surely</u> help next time.

In a Nutshell

- Action verbs are verbs that describe an action.
- Linking verbs are verbs that link a subject to its complement.
- Helping verbs are words such as *are*, *will*, and *had* that help a verb to express the past, present, and future.

PRACTICING 9

Underline the complete verb in the following sentences.

1. Dimitri had stopped his car a mile from camp.

2. Peter was waiting for her.

3. I will remember that picture.

4. She has begun to make the waffles.

5. They should have gone home earlier.

6. The accident was reported yesterday.

7. If only they had remained quiet!

8. The birds were chirping full force.

9. My father is sitting at the head of the table.

10. You should eat more fresh vegetables.

PRACTICING 10

Underline only the complete verb in the following sentences. Do not underline words that come between the helping verb and the main verb.

Example: They <u>had</u> never <u>helped</u> their neighbors.

1. You must occasionally hurry.

2. They have often traveled to a foreign country.

3. John should have deeply regretted his lie.

4. Few people can always smile when they are sad.

5. He must always have been the tallest in his class.

6. He had usually rented an apartment.

7. You could have quickly run across the street.

8. The man should have patiently waited.

9. The party has just been canceled.

10. Jane will never go swimming again.

Verbals

Verbals are words that look like verbs but do not act like verbs. Verbals are of three kinds: gerunds, participles, and infinitives. We'll look at each separately.

Gerunds

Gerunds are words that end in *-ing* and act as nouns. How can you tell if an *-ing* word is a gerund or a verb? Easy: look for the helping verb. For an *-ing* word to be a verb, it must have a helping verb. Look at these sentences:

We were swimming for fun.	**(were + *-ing* word = verb)**
Swimming is fun.	**(Swimming = subject = gerund)**
He is running in the Boston Marathon.	**(is + *-ing* word = verb)**
Running is good for you.	**(Running = subject = gerund)**

Apply the test for a subject by asking "Who?" or "What?" before the verb. "What" is good for you? Running; running = subject = gerund.

Weeding the garden can be hard work.

"What" can be hard work? Weeding; weeding = subject = gerund.

Another way to spot a gerund is to use the pronoun *it* in place of the suspect *-ing* word. If the *-ing* word is a gerund, this substitution is possible. If it is a verb, the substitution will seem ridiculous.

Swimming is fun.

It is fun.

The substitution makes sense: *swimming* is a gerund.

We were swimming for fun.

We were it for fun.

The sentence is ridiculous: *swimming* as used here is not a gerund.

PRACTICING 11

Rewrite the following sentences by turning the italicized verb into a gerund. As the example shows, you will have to add additional words.

Example: Scientists *are finding* cures for many diseases.

Finding cures for many diseases gives hope to the sick.
_____

1. Freddy *has been visiting* his grandparents.

_____

2. He *was using* a ruler to keep the lines straight.

_____

3. We *were hoping* for sunny weather.

_____

4. The children *were eating* candy.

_____

5. All year I *had been avoiding* my homework.

_____

6. John *was deciding* whether or not to join the team.

_____

7. When *was* Meg *wearing* a black hat?

_____

8. George and Ani *were watching* television.

_____

9. He *was kicking* the seat to annoy us.

_____

10. They *had been begging* us to paint the house green.

_____

PRACTICING 12

Mark *V* when the *-ing* word is used as a verb, and circle the helping verb. Mark *G* when the *-ing* word is used as a gerund.

1. _____ I am missing two assignments.

2. _____ All of us were wearing glasses.

3. _____ Marrying too young is not a good idea.

4. _____ Ted is marrying Jane.

5. _____ The directions are confusing.

6. _____ Winning the lottery would be nice.

7. _____ The screaming was eerie.

8. _____ I am counting on him.

9. _____ The officer was enforcing the law.

10. _____ Driving out West with my sister was fun.

Participles

Participles are words that look like verbs but act like adjectives, meaning that they describe. Present participles end in *-ing*. Past participles end in *-ed*. Here are some examples:

> Jack is dancing with Linda.

Here *is dancing* is a verb telling what Jack was doing.

> Jack is a dancing man.

Here *dancing* is a present participle describing the man Jack.

> We barbecued ribs for dinner.

Here *barbecued* is a verb telling what we did to the ribs.

> We ate barbecued ribs for dinner.

Here *barbecued* is a past participle describing ribs.

PRACTICING 13

In each of the following sentences, underline the participle.

Example: Jack has on a <u>battered</u> hat.

1. The chirping bird flew into a maple branch.

2. Howling winds kept us awake all night.

3. The sky looks like a painted wall.

4. My mother's darkened hair makes her look young.

5. None of the running horses belonged to the ranch.

6. Bowing her head, Georgia sighed.

7. A modified version of the bill passed the Assembly.

8. Watching an old movie, he fell asleep.

9. We had an uninterrupted view.

10. Bored neighbors came to watch the dancing.

Infinitives

Infinitives consist of *to* plus a verb. Infinitives never act as verbs; they always serve some other function. Study these examples:

> He wanted to disappear.

Here the infinitive *to disappear* tells what he wanted. The verb is *wanted*.

> He wanted a place to sleep.

Here the infinitive *to sleep* tells what kind of place. The verb is *wanted*.

> He waved to get her attention.

Here *to get* tells why he waved. The verb is *waved*.

Be careful not to confuse an infinitive with the preposition *to* followed by a noun or a pronoun.

Infinitive: Pete wanted <u>to walk</u>.

Preposition: Pete gave the apple <u>to Fred</u>.

In a Nutshell

- Verbals are words that look like verbs but do not act like verbs.

- Gerunds always end in *-ing* and act as nouns.

- Participles can end in *-ing* or *-ed*; they act as adjectives.

- An infinitive is *to* + a verb.

PRACTICING 14

Underline only the infinitives in the following sentences. Do not underline if the *to* is a preposition.

1. When do you plan to eat?

2. Margie gave her last dime to her sister.

3. Don't expect to see the lions.

4. We prefer to walk in the garden.

5. He whistled to the tune of "Yankee Doodle."

PRACTICING 15

In the following sentences, underline the verb and circle the infinitive.

Example: The wind <u>began</u> (to blow).

1. I am going to buy a new suit for my interview.

2. Every single student wanted to go to the game.

3. My boyfriend loves to ski.

4. I need to change the oil in my car.

5. It will be difficult to be as cheerful as Olivia.

6. Finally, I have learned how to drive a stick shift.

7. Everyone must leave in order to clear the hallways.

8. He refuses to lose weight.

9. I want to be alone.

10. Why don't you ask her to change your appointment?

Compound Subjects and Verbs

A sentence with more than one subject is said to have a **compound subject**. Here are some examples:

John and Peter fished.

The man and his son laughed.

My wife and I knew.

In the first sentence, *John* and *Peter* are both subjects of the verb *fished*. In the second the subjects are *man* and *son*. In the third the subjects are *wife* and *I*.

A sentence may also have more than one verb—called a **compound verb**. Here are some examples:

John fished and hunted.

The man talked and laughed.

I knew and understood.

The compound verbs are *fished* and *hunted* in the first sentence, *laughed* and *talked* in the second, and *knew* and *understood* in the third.

Naturally, compound subjects and verbs may occur in the same sentence:

> John, Peter, Tom, and Harry fished and hunted.

> The man and his son talked, laughed, and smiled.

> My wife and I knew, understood, and sympathized.

If you are like the rest of us, you often use such compound subjects and verbs in your everyday speech, perhaps without knowing their formal names. Recently a two-year-old we know tearfully blurted out this sentence after an accident:

> I tripped and fell.

When it was pointed out to her that she had just used a compound verb, she was neither consoled nor amused.

In a Nutshell

- A sentence with more than one subject has a compound subject.

- A sentence with more than one verb has a compound verb.

PRACTICING 16

Underline the compound subjects in the following sentences.

1. My teacher and I disagree.

2. My best friend and his wife came to dinner.

3. Fair weather and good company make the time fly.

4. Hope and love are both emotions.

5. Southern women and their diaries tell the story of the Civil War.

6. My dog, cat, and parakeet love one another.

7. Poetry and music are my twin loves.

8. Coffee, tea, and cookies were served.

9. Food and clothing are a big part of my budget.

10. A fool and his money are soon parted.

PRACTICING 17

Underline the compound verbs in the following sentences.

1. My heart sang and rejoiced at the victory.

2. He praised and rewarded my efforts.

3. Many people love and honor their roots.

4. The dog barked and howled all night.

5. She smiled and blew kisses to her fans.

6. I came and saw and conquered.

7. My husband scrimps and saves.

8. She said and did two different things.

9. The reporter talked and pointed to the map.

10. Terry dusted and vacuumed the room.

UNIT TEST

In the following sentences, underline the subject once and the complete verb twice.

1. The poster showed the beauty of the garden.

2. Timmy had been riding his bicycle for two hours.

3. Do you want to play football?

4. The clouds above the mountains looked white and fluffy.

5. Fifty packed years of experience have taught us much.

6. My whole life has been a miracle.

7. They should have been working.

8. Angie and George operate the scoreboard.

9. The car sputtered and stopped.

10. The broken lamp has not been of any use.

UNIT TALKING ASSIGNMENT

Choose a partner to whom you will ask the questions below and who must then write down an answer in a full sentence. Exchange roles and have your partner ask you the same questions, to which you will write your answers in complete sentences. Exchange papers. Circle the subjects and underline the verbs in your partner's sentences, while your partner does the same to yours. Do you agree on all the subjects and verbs? In case of disagreement, ask your instructor.

1. What is your favorite restaurant?
2. Why is it your favorite?
3. Where is it?
4. What is the decor like?
5. Whom do you go there with?
6. What kind of food does it serve?
7. Is it expensive?
8. How do the waiters act?
9. What are your favorite dishes?
10. How would you sum up your attitude toward this restaurant?

UNIT WRITING ASSIGNMENT

Use the sentences you wrote in the Unit Talking Assignment to write a paragraph on your favorite restaurant.

Building Sentences

> "Your ear for the language is the best judge
> of whether a clause makes sense or not and is
> therefore independent or dependent."

Every sentence must have a subject and a verb: There is no exception to this rule. But not every construction with a subject and verb is a sentence. It could be a dependent clause.

Dependent and Independent Clauses

A **clause** is a group of words with both a subject and a verb. If a clause makes sense on its own, it is called an **independent clause** and is a complete sentence. These are independent clauses and, therefore, complete sentences:

> They will pick up the dry cleaning.
>
> You can always go home for dinner.
>
> We are looking for a renter.

Each of the above has a subject (*they*, *you*, and *we*) and a verb (*will pick*, *go*, and *are looking*). Moreover, as your speaker's ear will tell you, each makes sense on its own.

However, what about the following?

> After you go to the bank.
>
> If it rains.
>
> Who has a steady income.

Each of the above clauses has a subject (*you*, *it*, and *who*) and a verb (*go*, *rains*, and *has*), but none makes complete sense. These are **dependent clauses**—a group of words with a subject and verb that must be connected to an independent clause to make sense.

> Pick up the dry cleaning after you go to the bank.
>
> You can always go to the movies if it rains.
>
> We are looking for a renter who has a steady income.

Your ear for the language is the best judge of whether a clause makes sense or not and is therefore independent or dependent. Most speakers, for example, can immediately hear the differences between the following pairs of clauses:

Dependent:	Since David moved.
Independent:	I haven't been backpacking.
Combined:	Since David moved, I haven't been backpacking.

Dependent:	After they sang.
Independent:	The audience applauded.
Combined:	After they sang, the audience applauded.

Dependent:	Which is my hometown.
Independent:	We stopped in Denver.
Combined:	We stopped in Denver, which is my hometown.

Many dependent clauses begin with a telltale sign—one of the following words. These words are called **relative pronouns** because they show how a dependent clause is related to a main clause.

who	whose	that
whom	which	

A dependent clause may also begin with one of these words, called **subordinating conjunctions**:

after	now that	unless
although	once	until
as if	provided that	when
because	rather than	whenever
before	since	where
even if	so that	wherever
even though	than	whether
if	that	while
in order that	though	why

Typically, it is these linking words that make a clause dependent. In fact, removing the subordinate conjunction changes a dependent clause into an independent clause. Here are some examples:

Dependent:	Since you left me.
Independent:	You left me.

Dependent:	Because you didn't study.
Independent:	You didn't study.

Dependent: While you were on vacation.

Independent: You were on vacation.

The obvious lesson to be learned is this: If you begin a sentence with one of the telltale words that make a clause dependent, be careful not to commit a dependent clause error.

In a Nutshell

- A clause is a group of words that contains a subject and verb.

- An independent clause makes sense on its own; a dependent clause does not.

- Only a clause that can stand by itself is a sentence.

PRACTICING 1

In the blanks provided, write *D* if the clause is dependent and *I* if the clause is independent.

1.   _____   Who darted across the street like lightning.

2.   _____   New brakes were needed.

3.   _____   The trial will begin in a week.

4.   _____   Because he was sad and depressed.

5.   _____   While walking home.

6.   _____   Though the soup was ready.

7.   _____   Since no book can provide all the answers.

8.   _____   That he never looked back.

9.   _____   If war could have solved the problem.

10. _____   Creative thinkers make good leaders.

PRACTICING 2

In each blank, write an independent clause that could complete the sentence.

Example: Because he was only seventeen, _he could not vote._

1. If you wear a badge with your name on it, _____

2. Before she moved to Idaho, _____

3. _____, where I found the wallet.

4. Unless you call before 2:00, _____

5. Whenever time passed slowly, _____

6. Mrs. Forsythe, who never spent a dime on Halloween

   treats, _____

7. Although getting exercise is important, _____

8. Because they won, _____

9. While visiting George, _____

10. Until television arrived, _____

Three Basic Sentence Types

There are three basic sentence types: simple, compound, and complex. All three sentence types are commonly used in writing and talking. We will discuss each separately.

The simple sentence

A **simple sentence** consists of a single independent clause. It is both the first sentence out of the mouth of babes as well as the workhorse of daily writing. First graders routinely write simple sentences such as these:

> Bobby fell down.

> Sally is my friend.

> I like my brother.

The simple sentence is commonly found in the Bible, where its simplicity is surprisingly powerful. Here, for example, is the first sentence of the Bible:

> In the beginning God created the heavens and the earth.

The simple sentence, in spite of its name, is not always simply written. Nor is it always short, crisp, and childlike. It can be expanded if it is given more than one subject or verb. Here are some examples:

Simple sentences with singular subjects:	My mother had no ear for music. My father had no ear for music.
Simple sentence with plural subject:	My mother and father had no ear for music.
Simple sentences with singular subject and singular verb:	The children laughed at the monkeys. They ran away from the tigers. They fed the goats.

Simple sentence with one subject and three verbs:	The children laughed at the monkeys, ran away from the tigers, and fed the goats.
Simple sentences with singular subjects and singular verbs:	The man laughed. The woman chuckled. The children giggled.
Simple sentence with three subjects and three verbs:	The man, woman, and children laughed, chuckled, and giggled.

Another way to expand the simple sentence is to add **modifiers**, which are words that describe and explain the subject or verb. Here are some examples:

Simple sentence:	Jim lives in Windsor.
First expansion:	Jim, a star basketball player, lives in Windsor.
Second expansion:	Jim, a star basketball player and an excellent student, lives in Windsor, which is in Canada, across from Detroit.

In a Nutshell

- The simple sentence consists of one independent clause.

- It can be expanded with multiple subjects and verbs or modifiers.

PRACTICING 3

Expand the simple sentences below by adding subjects, verbs, or modifiers.

Example: My father loves to fish.

Expanded by adding a modifier: My father, a retired firefighter, loves to fish.

Expanded by adding an additional subject and verb: My father and my uncle like to hike and love to fish.

1. My house is green. _____

_____

2. The man denied the story. _____

_____

3. Many people keep diaries. _____

_____

4. Sailing is fun. _____

_____

5. She is a generous woman. _____

_____

6. The train was late. _____

_____

7. He has a nickname. _____

_____

8. She went shopping. _____

_____

9. I could hardly believe my eyes. _____

_____

10. The room is full. _____

_____

The compound sentence

A **compound sentence** consists of two or more simple sentences joined by a coordinating conjunction. There are seven **coordinating conjunctions:** *and, but, for, or, nor, so, yet.* A comma is placed immediately before a coordinating conjunction. The simple sentences in a compound sentence should express ideas of equal importance. Here are some examples:

Simple: Face-lifts are not always successful. The operation is painful.

Compound: Face-lifts are not always successful, <u>and</u> the operation is painful.

Simple: He must pay the fine. He will go to jail.

Compound: He must pay the fine, <u>or</u> he will go to jail.

Simple: She was very bright. She didn't study. She got poor grades.

Compound: She was very bright, <u>but</u> she didn't study, <u>so</u> she got poor grades.

Notice that a comma comes immediately before the coordinating conjunction that joins the sentences.

In a Nutshell

- A compound sentence consists of two or more simple sentences joined by a coordinating conjunction.

- The coordinating conjunctions are: *and*, *but*, *for*, *or*, *nor*, *so*, *yet*.

- A comma is placed immediately before the joining conjunction.

PRACTICING 4

Use a coordinating conjunction to join these paired simple sentences into a compound sentence. Don't forget the comma.

Example: My mother hates exercising. My father loves it.

My mother hates exercising, but my father loves it.

1. The band played loudly. The audience enjoyed it.

   _____

2. I spoke to my neighbor. We made a date for lunch.

   _____

3. I went to aerobics class. I did 20 minutes on the treadmill. I'm exhausted.

   _____

4. Liza ran up the stairs. She made a telephone call.

   _____

5. I read the novel last night. I enjoyed it.

   _____

6. The dance was enjoyable. The students had a fine evening.

   _____

7. Bicarbonate of soda is good for an upset stomach. I often use it.

   _____

8. I reserved four tickets. That wasn't enough. I called for two more.

_____

9. We met at Luigi's. We had dinner. Molly never showed up.

_____

10. The bell rang. We filed out of the class.

_____

The complex sentence

The **complex sentence** consists of one independent clause joined to one or more dependent clauses. Unlike the compound sentence, which connects two equal ideas, the complex sentence emphasizes one idea over the others. The less important idea or ideas are said to be subordinate. The more important idea is expressed in the independent clause:

> My toe hurts because John stepped on it.

The hurting toe is the main idea; the less important idea is why it hurts—because John stepped on it.

Here is another example of a complex sentence—this one with one independent and two dependent clauses:

> Sculptures by Glenna Goodacre are very expensive, which means I will never own one, as much as I might want to.

The main idea here is that Glenna Goodacre's sculptures are expensive. The less important ideas are that the writer would like to buy one but can't because of the price.

Common sense and your ear for language will help you decide which of two ideas is more important and therefore belongs in the independent clause. Here are, for example, two sentences:

> I drank a cup of tea. I went to bed.

If you want to emphasize _going to bed_, put it in the independent clause:

> After drinking a cup of tea, I went to bed.

If you want to emphasize _drinking tea_, put it in the independent clause:

> Before I went to bed, I drank a cup of tea.

Exactly which idea you might choose to emphasize depends on what you want to say. Sometimes, however, it is clear which of two ideas is more important. Consider these two simple sentences:

> The _Titanic_ sank with a great loss of life. She struck an iceberg.

Common sense suggests that any complex sentence uniting these two ideas should emphasize the loss of life:

> After she struck an iceberg, the *Titanic* sank with a great loss of life.

The reason that the *Titanic* sank is secondary and belongs in the dependent clause.

Bear in mind the words that signal a dependent clause. You may wish to review the relative pronouns and subordinating conjunctions on page 22 before you do the exercises.

In a Nutshell

- A complex sentence consists of one independent clause joined to one or more dependent clauses.

- The more important idea is expressed in the independent clause.

PRACTICING 5

Join the following sentences in a complex sentence, using one of the linking words listed on page 22. Be sure to express ideas in their proper order of importance.

Example: My mother hates her work. She finds it boring.

My mother hates her work because she finds it boring.

1. She felt sorry for the beggar. She gave him money.

_____

2. The army retreated. It burned the bridges.

_____

3. We will proceed with the job. You object to the charges.

_____

4. You don't believe me. It is the truth.

_____

5. You have been gone. I have not been the same.

_____

6. The headmaster issued the uniforms. There was a complaint against them.

_____

7. You explain your behavior. I will report the incident.

_____

8. You were gone. The bill collector came.

_____

9. You will be admitted. You do well in the tests.

_____

10. The band stopped playing. The program was over.

_____

PRACTICING 6

Write a series of sentences on one of your favorite activities—something you really enjoy. Each sentence should be of the specific type listed below.

1. Simple sentence with more than one subject:

_____

2. Simple sentence with more than one verb:

_____

3. Simple sentence with modifiers:

_____

4. Two compound sentences:

(a) _____

_____

(b) _____

_____

5. Three complex sentences:

(a) _____

_____

(b) _____

_____

(c) _____

_____

> **PRACTICING 7**

Exchange papers with a classmate and discuss the sentences you wrote in Practicing 6. Help each other make any necessary corrections.

Sentence Variety

Writers seldom write in only one sentence type for the same reason that good cooks season their food with more than just salt. Any sentence pattern that is overused will quickly seem boring. Variety is the key to a good writing style and can be achieved easily if you use a mix of simple, compound, and complex sentences. Here is an example of a ho-hum passage:

> Rap music started during the 1970s. It comes from African chanting. It also comes from chatting. Rap music means "chat music." It contains. . . .

This passage consists of a string of simple sentences. Notice how it is immediately improved when the sentences are varied:

> Rap music, which started during the 1970s, comes from African chanting. It also comes from chatting. Rap music means "chat music," and it contains. . . .

This sort of sentence variation is exactly what you do instinctively in your everyday speech. It is what you must also try to do in your writing.

In a Nutshell

For variety, use all three sentence types—simple, compound, and complex—in your writing.

> **PRACTICING 8**

Rewrite each paragraph below to eliminate the choppy effect of too many simple sentences. Read the sentences aloud to determine the relationship between them. Then reduce the number of simple sentences by combining some into compound and complex sentences.

(1)

On Monday nothing seemed right. Friday Linda was pleased with her life. She had called her mother. Her mother had been feeling sick. On the phone she sounded chipper. Linda felt relieved. She decided to go camping in the mountains. Her friend had a cabin there. She would fish all weekend. She would be alone. She liked being alone. The weekend would cost little. She would only have to buy groceries for one. She had enough money. She had just gotten a paycheck. She would wear old clothes. She would lounge by the river. She would sleep late. There would be no alarm clock. Nobody would bother her. Linda thought, "Everything turns out for the best."

(2)

Most college students juggle the hours in their day. They play sports and go to parties. Many also have jobs. They try to include serving on committees. They perform volunteer work. They go to lectures. The many options do evoke a great deal of anxiety. The choices are unlimited. The hours are limited. Students feel pressured to get good grades. They feel pressured to experience life fully. They have to decide how much time they can spare outside of class and work for general enrichment. That decision is not always easy to make.

UNIT TEST

1. Write a simple sentence with modifiers about the clothing you are wearing today.

   _____

2. Write a compound sentence by connecting two simple sentences with "but."

   _____

   _____

3. Write a complex sentence beginning with "Although." Be sure to place a comma following the dependent clause.

   _____

   _____

4. Use the pattern of the following sentence, but change the words to create your own sentence on any topic of your choice: "I will never forget my Aunt Stella, because she was my favorite relative." What kind of sentence is this?

   _____

   _____

Identify each of the following sentences as simple, compound, or complex.

1. When John entered his astronomy class, he was embarrassed to find everyone staring at him. _____

2. Let's follow the instructions carefully, and then we'll compare what we've done with the picture. _____

3. If you hurry, you can probably catch her. _____

4. The umbrella, wet and dripping, stood in the corner of the hall. _____

5. Our neighborhood block party, which is held on Memorial Day, is always lots of fun. _____

6. Because we came late, we couldn't find seats together.

_____

UNIT TALKING ASSIGNMENT

Get together with two or three classmates to talk about your pet peeves, such as drivers who can't make up their minds, people who refuse to take their turns in lines, and teachers who wait until halfway through the semester to give the first exam. When one student is speaking, the others should write down some of the sentences. When everyone has discussed his or her pet peeve, take turns presenting and classifying the written sentences as simple, compound, or complex.

UNIT WRITING ASSIGNMENT

Using the ideas you accumulated during the Unit Talking Assignment, write about one of your pet peeves. Make a special effort to use sentence variety.

Avoiding Non-Sentences

> "If he blows up the world."
> "Fred is a flake no one likes him."
> "Last night I helped get supper, my potatoes were delicious."

You have already learned that a sentence is the same as an independent clause. It has a subject, a verb, and makes complete sense on its own. Non-sentences can be of two types—fragments and run-ons. We'll take up fragments first.

Fragments

A **fragment** is only part of a sentence. It is a "wannabe" sentence that lacks either subject or verb, and makes no sense; it fails to express a complete thought. Sometimes the omission occurs because the writer is "on a roll." It's fine to write fast and get all your thoughts down in a hurry, but then you must always proofread your work for errors.

Here are some examples of fragments that can occur in the rush of writing:

Has an 8:00 o'clock class.   **(missing subject)**

Joe's sweater.   **(missing verb)**

Especially when she is on a diet.   **(missing sense)**

Most of us speak in fragments every day without being misunderstood. Consider, for example, the exchange below:

Josh: Get your schedule yet?
Max: Sure did.
Josh: Any 8:00 o'clock classes?
Max: One. Psych.
Josh: Grim.
Max: I know. And with Skrebniski, too.

This conversation in fragments strikes the ear as typical of daily speech. Yet, in spite of the fragments, Max and Josh obviously still understand each other. Their exchange moves along smoothly, and neither interrupts the other for any clarification.

We have learned, however, that formal writing aims for a universal audience and therefore requires the use of **Standard English,** the English universally accepted by dictionaries and respected authorities, with a standard vocabulary and a standard grammar. Here is how Max and Josh's exchange would be written in Standard English:

Josh: Have you gotten your schedule yet?

Max: Yes, I have.

Josh: Do you have any 8:00 o'clock classes?

Max: I have one—psychology.

Josh: That's grim.

Max: I know. And the class is with Skrebniski, too.

The Standard English version may seem a little stiff, perhaps, compared to Max and Josh's informality. However, it is now understandable not only to Max and Josh, but to the millions of people around the world who read English.

In a Nutshell

A fragment is a "wannabe" sentence that lacks either a subject or verb and fails to express a complete thought.

PRACTICING 1

Identify the fragments in the list of constructions below. Mark *F* for a fragment and *S* for a complete sentence.

Example: __F__   Went to buy milk.

1.   _____   Hoping to score big.

2.   _____   He is a big man on campus.

3.   _____   Let me call you sweetheart.

4.   _____   To join the army.

5.   _____   Crying all the time.

6.   _____   Give me a few dollars.

7.   _____   I saw you in the garden.

8.   _____   Who's sorry now?

9. _____ Just in time.

10. _____ Because it's my decision.

Avoiding Sentence Fragments

A fragment can spring from one of several causes. If you learn to recognize these, you will be able to avoid fragments in your own writing.

Fragments caused by a missing subject

In the heat of writing, it is easy to write a verb but forget to write the subject. The result will be a fragment. Here are some examples:

> Kevin handed Marty two tickets for the playoffs. Then watched the look on his face.

> For appetizers we'll have chips and salsa. Also cheese and vegetables with dip.

In these examples, the writer mistakenly thought that the subject of the first sentence also applied to the second group of words. It does—but the second thought must be formally joined to the first by a conjunction, such as *and*. If you forget the conjunction, you must write the two thoughts as separate, complete sentences:

> Kevin handed Marty two tickets for the playoffs and watched the look on Marty's face.

or

> Kevin handed Marty two tickets for the playoffs. Then he watched the look on Marty's face.

> For appetizers we'll have chips and salsa, cheese, and vegetables with dip.

or

> For appetizers we'll have chips and salsa. We'll also have cheese and vegetables with dip.

In a Nutshell

Do not create a fragment by carelessly omitting the subject of the sentence.

PRACTICING 2

Correct the following fragments caused by a missing subject. You can either join the fragment to the sentence preceding it or rewrite it as a separate sentence.

Example: Maybe the universe is younger than we think. And was not caused by the Big Bang.

Joined: Maybe the universe is younger than we think and was not caused by the Big Bang.

Rewritten: Maybe the universe is younger than we think. Maybe it was not caused by the Big Bang.

1. Larry announced that he was going to Finland. Then showed me his ticket.

   _____

2. For plotting to kill Queen Elizabeth I, Sir Walter Raleigh was dropped from the list of the Queen's lovers. Also was beheaded.

   _____

   _____

3. Mario learned to ski. And loved the sport.

   _____

4. They prepared to entertain. But forgot to buy wine.

   _____

5. The car blew a tire. Spun around into a lamppost. And landed in a ditch.

   _____

   _____

6. I find Alice's rudeness to servers irritating. And tell her so.

   _____

7. Our bookkeeper did the ledger. But didn't do the spreadsheets.

   _____

8. Mr. Gibson was always talking about politics. And was himself quite a politician.

   _____

   _____

9. He served a wonderful dinner. But burned the dessert.

_____

10. Cathy was sorry. Or at least said she was.

_____

Fragments due to -ing words

Some fragments are triggered by an _-ing_ word, such as _singing_. Here are some examples:

> They celebrated. Dancing in the street.

> The plane landed. Skidding to a halt.

Why beginning with an _-ing_ word often leads to a fragment is something of a puzzle. Possibly, the writer mistakes the _-ing_ word for a full verb, but it isn't. As you know from Unit 1, an _-ing_ word can only be a verb in a sentence if it is paired with a helping verb.

To correct a fragment due to an _-ing_ word, either join it to the sentence that went before (use a comma to set off the first part of the sentence), or rewrite it as a separate sentence:

> They celebrated, dancing in the street.

> > or

> They celebrated. They were dancing in the street.

> The plane landed, skidding to a halt.

> > or

> The plane landed. It skidded to a halt.

In a Nutshell

Be careful of creating a fragment with an _-ing_ word.

PRACTICING 3

Correct the _-ing_ fragments by rewriting the sentences below.

1. My parents wouldn't let me study the trumpet. Insisting that I should learn to play the piano.

_____

_____

2. He spent two summers on a farm. Picking vegetables in the heat of the day.

_____

_____

3. The coach lifted curfew. Believing the team members could discipline themselves.

_____

_____

4. His handwriting is filled with sharp points and angles. Classifying him as a mean and stingy person.

_____

_____

5. The director carefully observed the dancers. Looking for signs of exceptional talent.

_____

_____

6. He loves to read. Spending many hours in an armchair.

_____

7. He attended to his father's business. Working long hours every day.

_____

8. She was the star of the soccer team. Having scored the most goals.

_____

9. He proposed to her one day. Getting down on his knee.

_____

10. Many movies are violent. Appealing to the resentment people feel.

_____

Fragments due to the incorrect use of infinitives

A third common type of fragment is triggered by the incorrect use of infinitives (*to* + verb). Here is an example:

I am taking karate lessons. To build up my strength.

John went to a movie. To get his mind off exams.

As before, you can correct this type of fragment by either joining it to the sentence before, or rewriting it as a separate and complete sentence:

Joined: I am taking karate lessons to build up my strength.

Rewritten: I am taking karate lessons. I want to build up my strength.

Joined: John went to a movie to get his mind off exams.

Rewritten: John went to a movie. He needed to get his mind off exams.

Note that you could also move the clause containing the infinitive to the beginning of the combined sentence. If you do this, put a comma after the main clause.

To build up my strength, I am taking karate lessons.

To get his mind off exams, John went to a movie.

In a Nutshell

Watch out for fragments caused by the incorrect use of infinitives.

PRACTICING 4

Correct the following *to* fragments by either joining them to the sentences before or rewriting them as separate sentences.

1. The students took out state educational loans. To get money at a low interest rate.

   _____

   _____

2. I, too, would like a wife. To tend to my every want and slightest need.

   _____

   _____

3. We screen our calls through our message machine. To avoid telephone marketers.

   _____

   _____

4. I bought some property outside of Phoenix. To build a cabin some day.

_____

_____

5. I used to live in San Antonio, Texas. To make a long story short.

_____

6. He took the train home. To avoid the heavy traffic.

_____

7. She read a novel. To while away the time.

_____

8. She took a summer job. To earn money for college.

_____

9. You need a key. To start the engine.

_____

10. He exercised all summer. To make the football team.

_____

Fragments due to dependent words

You have learned about fragments caused by omitted subjects, *-ing* words, and the incorrect use of infinitives. You have also learned two ways of correcting fragments—by joining the fragment to the sentence before or by rewriting the fragment as a separate sentence.

We come now to a fourth kind of fragment. This one is triggered by the misuse of relative pronouns and subordinate conjunctions, both of which we covered in Unit 2. This fourth type of fragment is corrected in only one way: by joining it to the sentence before. Here is a list of relative pronouns that can cause fragments:

who	whose	that
whom	which	

Here are examples of fragments caused by unconnected relative pronouns:

We inspected the attic. <u>Which</u> had become a dumping ground for excess furniture.

Next month we must pay tribute to Coach Peters. <u>Who</u> helped us win the trophy.

Here are the corrections:

> We inspected the attic, <u>which</u> had become a dumping ground for excess furniture.

> Next month we must pay tribute to Coach Peters, <u>who</u> helped us win the trophy.

As you can see, both fragments were corrected by joining them to the sentence before. Indeed, both were caused by the writer's use of a period instead of a comma.

Similarly, a fragment can be caused by the misuse of a subordinate conjunction. Here is a list of subordinate conjunctions:

after	although	as if
because	before	even if
even though	if	in order that
now that	once	provided that
rather than	since	so that
than	that	though
unless	until	when
whenever	where	wherever
whether	while	why

Here some examples of fragments caused by unconnected subordinate conjunctions:

> Even though society seems to be increasingly concerned. Crime keeps rising.

> After the flood subsided. The corn started to grow again.

To correct such fragments, simply join them to the neighboring sentence:

> Even though society seems to be increasingly concerned, crime keeps rising.

> The corn started to grow again after the flood subsided.

Note that if the dependent clause comes first, it is separated from the independent clause by a comma:

Incorrect: Since it was our anniversary. We ordered lobster.

Correct: Since it was our anniversary, we ordered lobster.

But: We ordered lobster since it was our anniversary.

In a Nutshell

Subordinate conjunctions and relative pronouns can trigger sentence fragments. Correct these fragments by joining them to a neighboring sentence.

PRACTICING 5

Rewrite the following fragments by joining them to a neighboring sentence.

1. We shop at Piggly-Wiggly. Although I prefer Dominick's for meats.

   _____

2. The words acquired new meaning. When he found out they were spoken by Abraham Lincoln.

   _____

   _____

3. Now, let's look at the words *bull* and *cow*. Which are simply male and female equivalents.

   _____

   _____

4. Stop and take a rest. If your breathing becomes labored.

   _____

5. My favorite restaurant is the Fireside Inn. Although it isn't cheap.

   _____

6. The hills were alive with the voices of people. Whose laughter rang across the valley.

   _____

   _____

7. He plans several sports. Since he is quite athletic.

   _____

   _____

8. I want to leave the hustle and bustle of city life. Where every decision is one more frustration.

_____

_____

9. He worked hard and studied until midnight every night. In order to make the Dean's List.

_____

_____

10. Get one large pizza. Rather than two medium ones.

_____

Fragments due to added details

Details added to a sentence can also cause a fragment. Beware of the words listed below. They often lead to added-detail fragments.

especially	including
except	not even
particularly	such as
in addition	for example

Here are three examples of fragments caused by added details:

The entire neighborhood was up in arms. Except the Johnson sisters.

The expedition leader warned of many hardships. Among them freezing weather, lack of food, and difficult terrain.

Pottery made by the Acoma has very bold geometric designs. For example, horizontal and vertical lines, triangles, and diamonds.

To correct a fragment caused by added details, simply attach the details to the previous sentence (using a comma to set off the added details) and add any necessary words:

The entire neighborhood was up in arms, except the Johnson sisters.

The expedition leader warned of many hardships, among them freezing weather, lack of food, and difficult terrain.

If the additional detail fragment is long, you can make it into a separate sentence:

Pottery made by the Acoma has very bold geometric designs. These designs feature horizontal and vertical lines, triangles, and diamonds.

In a Nutshell

Details added to a sentence as an afterthought can cause a fragment. Correct the fragment by connecting it to the previous sentence or by turning it into a complete sentence of its own.

PRACTICING 6

Correct the following fragments caused by added details by joining them to the sentence before.

1. Some of my favorite people are a little eccentric. For example, the woman who wears an evening gown to feed the pigeons.

   _____

   _____

2. Certain languages are more musical than others. Among them Italian and Spanish.

   _____

   _____

3. She received many gifts. Tickets to a Hawks game, a bracelet, and a couple of CDs.

   _____

   _____

4. No parent always makes the right decision. Not even with the best intentions.

   _____

   _____

5. We encountered some minor difficulties. Including locking the keys in the car.

   _____

   _____

6. I have an early class next quarter. English 101 with Henderson.

   _____

7. The girls kept getting into trouble at the bus stop. Except for Mary, an A student.

_____

_____

8. Students should be encouraged to become intimate with their books. Even writing in the margins of pages.

_____

_____

9. The Boston Pops always puts on a great July 4th celebration. With fireworks and a cannon.

_____

_____

10. A good leader never leaves his followers without hope. Especially in times of serious trouble.

_____

_____

Run-on Sentences

A **run-on sentence** is actually two sentences mistaken for one. There are two main types of run-on sentences: the fused sentence and the comma splice.

The **fused sentence** consists of two sentences joined—or fused—without any punctuation between them:

We toured General Grant's home it is in Illinois.

Here is how the sentence should be written:

We toured General Grant's home. It is in Illinois.

The second type of run-on sentence is the **comma splice**—two full sentences separated by a comma instead of a period:

The steak was gray and tough, the eggs tasted like rubber.

Here is the sentence, corrected:

The steak was gray and tough. The eggs tasted like rubber.

PRACTICING 7

In the blanks provided, indicate *FS* if the run-on sentence is fused and *CS* if it is spliced.

Example: __CS__ She is beautiful, she is too thin.

1. _____ Don't wait another minute send your money now.

2. _____ He must attend class on Wednesday, a test will be given.

3. _____ Raspberries are tasty, they are expensive.

4. _____ You may be able to live on love you definitely can't retire on it.

5. _____ Scorpions are wary they rely on their natural camouflage to protect them from enemies.

6. _____ Mark Blumenstein is a modern artist he uses saws, gas nozzles, and scythe blades in his sculptures.

7. _____ Get relief from allergies use a steam inhalator.

8. _____ It was cold, windy, and dark the fish didn't hit.

9. _____ People from all walks of life play softball it is our most democratic pastime.

10. _____ She wore a black turtleneck everyone wanted to know where she had bought it.

Correcting run-on sentences

There are four ways to correct run-on sentences. Take, for example, this one:

> Frank is outgoing Jeff is timid.

To correct it, you can do one of the following:

1. Put a period at the end of the first sentence:

   Frank is outgoing. Jeff is timid.

2. Put a semicolon at the end of the first sentence:

   Frank is outgoing; Jeff is timid.

3. Put a coordinating conjunction (with a comma before it) at the end of the first sentence:

   Frank is outgoing, but Jeff is timid.

4. Use a subordinating conjunction:

Frank is outgoing though Jeff is timid.

or

Though Frank is outgoing, Jeff is timid.

In a Nutshell

Two sentences run together as one create a run-on sentence. To correct a run-on sentence, do one of the following:

• Put a period between them.

• Put a semicolon between them.

• Put a coordinating conjunction between them. (Don't forget the comma.)

• Use a subordinating conjunction.

PRACTICING 8

Correct the following run-ons in all four possible ways.

1. He sent a dozen roses she still didn't forgive him.

Insert a period: _____

_____

Insert a semicolon: _____

_____

Insert a coordinating conjunction and comma: _____

_____

Insert a subordinating conjunction (with comma if needed): ____

_____

2. I've always wanted a pickup truck it's only a matter of time until I get one.

Insert a period: _____

_____

Insert a semicolon: _____

_____

Insert a coordinating conjunction and comma:_____

_____

Insert a subordinating conjunction (with comma if needed): ____

_____

3. It rained all day, the yard was one big puddle.

Insert a period: _____

_____

Insert a semicolon: _____

_____

Insert a coordinating conjunction and comma:_____

_____

Insert a subordinating conjunction (with comma if needed): ____

_____

4. Bring nametags and pens Mary always forget them.

Insert a period: _____

_____

Insert a semicolon: _____

_____

Insert a coordinating conjunction and comma:_____

_____

Insert a subordinating conjunction (with comma if needed): ____

_____

5. The children looked for shells their mother watched that
they didn't wander far.

Insert a period: _____

_____

Insert a semicolon: _____

_____

Insert a coordinating conjunction and comma:_____

_____

Insert a subordinating conjunction (with comma if needed): ____

_____

PRACTICING 9

Correct the following run-on sentences.

1. Today is my birthday I still feel young.

   _____

   _____

2. Rico wanted to go on vacation, his boss demanded the report by tomorrow.

   _____

   _____

3. Bright red lipstick looks gaudy it isn't popular this summer.

   _____

   _____

4. Our plane was delayed, the fog was too thick.

   _____

   _____

5. Botany is difficult for me it involves much memory work.

   _____

   _____

6. A computer is a mystery, I can't even imagine how it functions.

   _____

   _____

7. My first date with Felice was a disaster, she wanted to dance and I am a klutz.

   _____

   _____

8. I made a plum pie it was juicy and sweet.

   _____

   _____

9. I picked up my coat and ran to the front door my dad was patiently waiting.

     _____

     _____

10. We had to watch ten minutes of silly trailers the main movie did not begin until 7:15.

     _____

     _____

PRACTICING 10

Correct the following run-on sentences.

1. Chris has a good sense of humor he often laughs at himself.

     _____

     _____

2. Sandra is a striking child, with jet black ringlets framing her face, she looks like her mother.

     _____

     _____

3. The male butterfly attracts a mate by fluttering around and showing off his strategy doesn't always work.

     _____

     _____

4. The police log shows burglaries are down car theft is up, though.

     _____

     _____

5. Caterpillars are one of nature's great illusions who would ever think that these wormlike creatures become such beauties?

     _____

     _____

6. Sherry is totally unreliable, sometimes she arrives an hour or two late.

     _____

     _____

7. You cannot avoid cold germs simply by hiding from everyone, a better way is to strengthen your resistance.

_____

_____

8. I decided to change my approach I would pretend total indifference to her.

_____

_____

9. All of us like to show off at times no one is immune to the human need for attention.

_____

_____

10. Lip readers read each word slowly, on the other hand, speed readers drop diagonally down the page to catch the main ideas.

_____

_____

PRACTICING 11

A. Some of the sentences below are correct; others contain fragments or run-ons. If the sentence is correct, write *C* in the blank. If the sentence is incorrect, write *NC* in the blank and rewrite the sentence to correct the error.

1. I arrived at the park at noon, the sun was directly overhead and a few random clouds were scattered across the sky. _____

_____

_____

2. I brought nothing with me except a pen and notebook for recording my thoughts I did not want to spoil the park's natural beauty with anything from the outside world. _____

_____

_____

3. Other people had also decided to visit the park that day, we paid no attention to each other. _____

_____

_____

4. I stood on a grassy knoll. Where I could observe and absorb everything around me. _____

_____

_____

5. To the left of me was a small grove of orange trees. Including a tree so gnarled that it looked as if it had been transplanted from a witch's garden. _____

_____

_____

_____

6. Everywhere else, all I could see were mountains, mountains, mountains. _____

_____

_____

7. As I walked toward the orange grove, I heard different birds calling to one another. _____

_____

_____

8. Birds have a freedom that humans do not possess.   The freedom to soar above the ground and see the world from a different perspective. _____

_____

_____

9. I picked an orange from a low branch, peeled it, and squeezed the juice into my mouth._____

_____

_____

10. The sweetness trickled from my lips, it seemed like drops of some magical potion. _____

_____

_____

B. The following paragraph contains fragments and run-ons. Correct each error by one of the methods described in this unit.

Two years had passed since I had last seen my grandmother. During this time, her condition had worsened, now she was completely bedridden. No longer able to get up and walk. She babbled without making sense, she had no idea who I was. Her gray eyes stared vacantly. As if she were half in another world unknown to me. All I could do was smile at her and hold her hand. Yet, I was struck by the fact that even in this hopelessly deteriorated state, she seemed to want to communicate with me she wanted a human connection. I decided she was still my kind, beautiful grandmother inside, no matter how she appeared on the outside. Today I wonder what it will be like when I am old. Personally, I hope I don't live long enough to be in such a deteriorated condition. Unable to recognize loved ones. How frustrating it must be to be senile. To repeat the same questions and to remember nothing. Still, maybe science will some day find a cure for extreme senility, I hope so.

UNIT TEST

After each sentence write *F* for fragment, *CS* for comma splice, and *FS* for fused sentences. Then correct each error. (Note: One of the sentences contains two errors.)

1. Diogenes was not a degenerate or a beggar he was a philosopher and poet. _____

_____

_____

2. Macaroni and cheese are quick and easy meals. Also spaghetti. _____

_____

_____

3. Political correctness has its down side, it may stop any honest debate about sensitive subjects. _____

_____

_____

4. I love our family farm. Because all of my childhood memories are connected with this piece of land. _____

_____

_____

5. History teaches us that rebels were often right they were not always crazy or radical. Consider, for example, George Washington, Luther, and Galileo. _____

_____

_____

_____

6. Most Americans get their news from television they read newspapers only for sports and human interest stories. _____

_____

_____

7. Rollerblading is good exercise you should wear kneepads when you're first learning. _____

_____

_____

8. The ice skater gracefully lifted his partner above his head the audience gasped. _____

_____

_____

9. The health food store closed, I guess it wasn't making

money. _____

_____

_____

10. We drove from Cleveland to Pittsburgh and back. Filling up

on gas only once. _____

_____

_____

UNIT TALKING ASSIGNMENT

Some of the sentences in the following paragraphs are correct, but some are fragments or run-ons. Correct all the incorrect sentences. Then team up with a classmate, exchange books, and check each other's work. Discuss any sentences on which you disagree.

I am a file clerk in the office of one of Denny's restaurants, I am required to file correctly. While this process may seem easy, it can actually become a real problem. If the proper filing rules are not followed. Nothing is more confusing and time wasting than lost files.

Here are some basic filing rules to follow: First, you need to know the correct order of the letters in the alphabet. Something you should have learned in grade school. Second, a file clerk must know that for each of the 26 letters there is a file cut, the file cut is the label part that extends above the rest of the file. These file cuts are right, left, and middle. Third, before you put files in a filing cabinet, you must take the time to alphabetize them so you don't have to jump back and forth. From drawer to drawer. Fourth, while filing, you must never rush otherwise you are likely to misfile. Which may cause big trouble because lost files are hard to find later.

Finally, the order of filing is important and can be tricky. For instance, you must file by a person's last name. If two people have the same last name, then use the first name to distinguish between them. To stay in proper alphabetical order. For instance, "John Smith," comes after "Agnes Smith." Furthermore, a space in a name is treated as if the space were not there, for instance, "De Lang" precedes "Derring." Following these simple rules lessens the risk of making filing errors, and in the long run they will save you time and energy.

UNIT WRITING ASSIGNMENT

Using freewriting, brainstorming, clustering, or any other method of prewriting, write about one of these subjects:

1. The person you are that others seldom see
2. Your attitude toward practical jokes
3. Someone you think is terribly funny

Verbs—An Overview

"They had danced when they were younger."

Verbs can be troublesome. Part of the problem is that we don't speak and write verbs the same way. In speech we sometimes drop the tense endings of verbs when we shouldn't, as in this sentence:

> She talk too much.

Or, we add an ending when we shouldn't:

> They talks too much.

In the first sentence, since *she* is singular, the verb must also be singular—*talks*. In the second sentence, since *they* is plural, the verb must also be plural—*talk*.

You can make these mistakes in everyday speech—we all occasionally do—and be forgiven. You should not, however, make them in writing. The standards for grammar are more strict in writing than in speech, meaning that you must always write verb tenses correctly.

There is good news: You already know more about verb tenses than you realize.

Twelve Tenses

English has twelve tenses. Of these twelve tenses, the most widely used are the simple present, past, and future. Here is a formal list of all the tenses and their functions:

Name of tense	How it is used	Example
Present	For actions that are now and ongoing	I <u>dance</u>. Bill <u>dances</u>.
Simple past	For actions that took place in the past and do not extend into the present	We <u>danced</u> all night.
Future	For actions that will happen some time after now	I <u>will dance</u> at your wedding.

Name of tense	How it is used	Example
Present perfect	For actions that started in the past and have been completed in the present	I <u>have</u> just <u>finished</u> dancing.
Past perfect	For actions that were completed in the past before another action took place.	Amazingly, she <u>had</u> often <u>danced</u> with him before he became president.
Future perfect	For actions that will happen in the future before some other specific future action	The couple <u>will have danced</u> twice before you leave.
Present progressive	For actions that are still in progress	They <u>are dancing</u> in the park.
Past progressive	For actions that were in progress in the past	She <u>was dancing</u> like a gypsy.
Future progressive	For future actions that will take place continuously	He <u>will be dancing</u> with you.
Present perfect progressive	For actions that started in the past and continue into the present	Madame Francois <u>has been dancing</u> lately.
Past perfect progressive	For actions that were in progress in the past before another past action took place	Everyone <u>had been dancing</u> until the music stopped.
Future perfect progressive	For actions that continue to take place before some other future action	The dancing <u>will have been going on</u> a long time before you have to choose a winner.

Scanning this table of tenses should make you appreciate your instinctive sense of grammar. Most people who speak English fluently cannot name all the twelve tenses but still know how to use them. This is all the more remarkable because many of us rarely, if ever, use some of these tenses. Sometimes months, even years, go by before we use the future perfect progressive. When we do use it, we do so unconsciously. Grammar, as we have said repeatedly in this book, is largely a built-in skill as natural and automatic as walking.

Present Tense Endings

In Standard English you must use the correct endings with verbs. You cannot use a plural ending with a singular subject, or a singular ending with a plural subject. Here are the correct endings for regular verbs in the present tense:

PRESENT TENSE—SINGULAR

Incorrect	**Correct**
I walks	I walk
you walks	you walk
he ⎫	he ⎫
she ⎬ walk	she ⎬ walks
it ⎭	it ⎭

PRESENT TENSE—PLURAL

Incorrect	**Correct**
we walks	we walk
you walks	you walk
they walks	they walk

Present tense problems

There are two kinds of problems that commonly occur with verbs in the present tense.

1. Dropped -s/-es endings for *he*, *she*, and *it*.
   Incorrect: She walk home the long way.
   Correct: She walks home the long way.

   Incorrect: Bob play the piano for relaxation.
   Correct: Bob plays the piano for relaxation.

   Incorrect: He wash the kitchen floor once a week.
   Correct: He washes the kitchen floor once a week.

2. Unnecessary -s/-es for *we*, *you*, and *they*.
   Incorrect: We plays hard every day.
   Correct: We play hard every day.

   Incorrect: You checks out everything.
   Correct: You check out everything.

   Incorrect: They watches out for everybody.
   Correct: They watch out for everybody.

Problems with dropped and added endings occur, as we said, because we are less precise in our speech than we must be in our writing. If you regularly make such errors in your speech, your ear may not be particularly helpful in catching them. In that case you should simply memorize the correct endings. When we think we see a situation where your ear for spoken language might trick you, we will warn you with an "Ear Alert" such as this one.

PRACTICING 1

In the blank provided, mark *C* if the verb is correct and *NC* if it is not.

Example: __NC__ He always whistle in the dark.

1. _____ Jim and I live on Broadway.

2. _____ We love baseball.

3. _____ This restaurant need remodeling.

4. _____ Franny own two cats.

5. _____ She forget who her teacher is.

6. _____ Women wants good careers nowadays.

7. _____ I hope Harry washes his car.

8. _____ My computer save me lots of time.

9. _____ Aunt Elsie walks two miles every day.

10. _____ Jake and Mervin spends too much time watching television.

PRACTICING 2

Underline the correct verb.

Example: The bus (<u>stops</u>, stop) in front of Mary's house.

1. The waiters (wears, wear) purple suspenders.

2. A big white dog (sit, sits) on the porch swing.

3. All the girls (wants, want) to pierce their ears.

4. The lemons (need, needs) to be grated.

5. Two fleecy clouds (drifts, drift) across the sky.

6. Suzy and I (prefers, prefer) to eat later.

7. We (believe, believes) that country life is better than city life.

8. The schools (deserve, deserves) the most modern libraries.

9. Greg and Karin (promises, promise) to make the punch.

10. Several movie stars (lead, leads) troubled lives.

PRACTICING 3

In the passage that follows, strike out any incorrect verb and write the correct form above it.

1. Mrs. Farrow, our next-door neighbor, hate dogs. 2. Anytime she hear our dog bark, she yell at him, "Shut up, you ugly mutt." 3. I suppose people like this neighbor dislikes pets because they never had a pet of their own. 4. I feel sorry for Mrs. Farrow because she believe that dogs exists just to be yelled at and never to be treated as friends. 5. Mrs. Farrow live alone, and it seem to me that a dog could be excellent company for her if she would just change her attitude.

Past Tense Endings

Here are the correct endings for regular singular verbs in the past tense:

PAST TENSE—SINGULAR

Incorrect	**Correct**
I walk	I walked
you walk	you walked
he	he
she } walk	she } walked
it	it

Here are the correct endings for regular plural verbs in the past tense:

PAST TENSE—PLURAL

Incorrect	**Correct**
we walk	I walked
you walk	you walked
they walk	he, she, it walked

With both singular and plural verbs, we can be careless in our speech and drop the -ed ending. But in writing, you must always use the -ed ending with regular verbs in the past tense.

Incorrect: I hike there yesterday.
Correct: I hiked there yesterday.

Incorrect: She bake a pie last week.
Correct: She baked a pie last week.

PRACTICING 4

In the blank at the end of each sentence, write the past tense of the italicized verb.

Example: Only his nose *remain* uncovered. <u>remained</u>

1. The giggling clown *twist* his nose. _____

2. We *decide* to match him dollar for dollar. _____

3. To my deep sorrow, John *believe* a stranger, not me. _____

4. She barely *manage* to wheel her bicycle into the garage. _____

5. They *last* much longer than expected. _____

6. They *deliver* the paper two days late. _____

7. Fred and Merv *order* two big pizzas. _____

8. I *decide* to spare myself much grief by breaking up with Sally. _____

9. Two or three days ago the weather *change* abruptly. _____

10. Disregarding the sign, he *park* in the Disabled Section. _____

Problems with -ing verbs

Verbs ending in *-ing* describe an action that is either happening now or is ongoing. As you learned in Unit 1, all *-ing* verbs need a helping verb.

She is studying in the library.

She was studying in the library.

She has been studying in the library.

She had been studying in the library, but now she studies in her dorm.

Two kinds of problems can occur with *-ing* verbs:

1. *Be* or *been* is used instead of the correct helping verb.

    Incorrect: She be studying in the library.

    Correct: She is studying in the library.

    or

    She has been studying in the library.

Incorrect:	She been studying in the library.
Correct:	She was studying in the library.

or

She has been studying in the library.

2. The helping verb is completely omitted:

Incorrect:	They pretending not to know.
Correct:	They are pretending not to know.
	They were pretending not to know.
	They have been pretending not to know.
	They had been pretending not to know.

Both kinds of errors can confuse and mislead a reader. *She has been studying in the library* is more precise than *She be studying in the library*. With the helping verb missing, we can't tell whether an action is ongoing, or has already gone on but is now over. *They pretending not to know* is therefore fuzzier than *They have been pretending not to know*. Be alert to the possibility of both errors.

PRACTICING 5

Rewrite the following sentences to correct the misuse of *be* or *been* or to insert the missing helping verb.

Example: The children be screaming in the room.

The children are screaming in the room.

Example: They having a sale at Macy's.

They are having a sale at Macy's.

1. My family be wanting to move to Baltimore.

_____

2. She telling her daughter not to marry Bud.

_____

3. Amy putting up with her roommate's messy ways.

_____

4. How she be doing at her job?

_____

5. Frank wishing he were class president.

_____

6. They be listening to three speakers praising Amway.

   _____

7. Mr. Goldman watching the movie *Working Girls* when the storm hit.

   _____

   _____

8. Every generation be creating its own music.

   _____

9. Mitch pushing the idea of creating a band.

   _____

10. We be expecting too much from that motor.

    _____

PRACTICING 6

Underline the correct form of the verb.

1. She (be, has been) studying without proper lighting.

2. Our art class (hoping, is hoping) to go on a museum field trip.

3. The mechanic at the gas station (had been working, working) on Pete's jeep.

4. Most of the children (be, are) asking for hot dogs.

5. Raquel (has been, be) trying out for the swimming team.

6. Every time the teacher (be, was) reading from his notes, we fell asleep.

7. I (was expecting, expecting) to have to show my ID.

8. Lindsay (be, has been) feeling much better today.

9. We constantly (be, are) hearing that the family is in trouble.

10. Actually, Dad (trying, was trying) to reach you by phone.

Difficult Verbs

Verbs can be hard to master. Few, though, are harder to master than the three verbs we probably use more than any others in the language: *be, have* and *do.* Not only are these verbs in their own right, but they are also commonly used as helping verbs. (Try saying a few sentences without *be*, *have* and *do* and see how much you miss them.) We'll treat each one separately.

To be

To be is commonly used both as a verb on its own and as a helping verb. Here is a listing of the forms of the verb *to be*:

PRESENT TENSE—SINGULAR *to be*

Incorrect

I be, I ain't

you be, you ain't

he
she } be/ain't
it

Correct

I am, I am not

you are, you are not

he
she } is/is not
it

PRESENT TENSE—PLURAL *to be*

Incorrect

we be, we ain't

you be, you ain't

they be, they ain't

Correct

we are, we are not

you are, you are not

they are, they are not

PAST TENSE—SINGULAR *to be*

Incorrect

I were

you was

he
she } were
it

Correct

I was

you were

he
she } was
it

PAST TENSE—PLURAL *to be*

Incorrect

we was

you was

they was

Correct

we were

you were

they were

Ear Alert

As you can see—indeed as you already know from repeated use—*to be* is an irregular verb. As both a verb and a helping verb, it is often incorrectly spoken. All of the following sentences, for example, are wrong, even if your ear tells you otherwise.

Incorrect	**Correct**
I ain't going to do it.	I am not going to do it.
Absence be the reason he gets poor grades.	Absence is the reason he gets poor grades.
You was right about her.	You were right about her.

If you commonly use the incorrect forms in your daily speech, be especially careful not to trust your ear with *to be*. Instead, memorize its correct forms.

PRACTICING 7

The following passage contains several errors in the use of the verb *to be*. In the space provided, rewrite the passage, correcting all errors. (Hint: you should find ten errors.)

My car be a ten-year-old Chevy. I bought it for $300.00 and I ain't going to sell it because it be a great car. Hank, my buddy, and I worked all last summer to improve the car and make it run. We be proud of our work because the car be the best in our school. The paint job be bright red. The other kids are jealous of us because they ain't smart enough to fix up a car the way we fixed up ours. Hank be the kind of friend who helps me with keeping up this car. It be good to have such a loyal buddy, ain't that so?

_____

_____

_____

_____

_____

_____

_____

_____

_____

_____

_____

To have

To have, like *to be*, is commonly used both as a verb and as a helping verb. Like *to be*, it is also an irregular verb. Its main forms follow.

PRESENT TENSE—SINGULAR *to have*

Incorrect	Correct
I has	I have
you has	you have
he	he
she } have	she } has
it	it

PRESENT TENSE—PLURAL *to have*

Incorrect	Correct
we has	we have
you has	you have
they has	they have

PAST TENSE—SINGULAR *to have*

Incorrect	Correct
I has	I had
you has	you had
he	he
she } have	she } had
it	it

PAST TENSE—PLURAL *to have*

Incorrect	Correct
we has	we had
you has	you had
they has	they had

Like *to be*, *to have* is so often misused in daily speech that you should be cautious about trusting your ear to judge its correctness. The sentences below, for example, are all incorrect:

Ear Alert

> She have a problem.

> He have on a new coat.

> They has a quarrel yesterday.

Here are the correct forms:

> She has a problem.

He has on a new coat.

They had a quarrel yesterday.

PRACTICING 8

In the following sentences, fill in the correct form of the verb *to have*.

Example: She <u>has</u> to go.

1. Mary _____ a pet collie.

2. You _____ to stop saying that.

3. Mr. Ward _____ the only blue house on the street.

4. You _____ my only copy, and I must _____ it back.

5. I _____ got to let go of her, and she _____ to understand why.

6. _____ he said anything to you about it?

7. Where _____ you been?

8. He _____ borrowed by car for the last time.

9. No one _____ a right to say that.

10. I _____ many friends, but she _____ only one.

To do

The verb *to do*, like *to be* and *to have*, is used both as a main verb and as a helping verb. It is so common to both writing and speech as to be found nearly everywhere. Here are its correct forms:

PRESENT TENSE—SINGULAR *to do*

Incorrect	**Correct**
I does	I do
you does	you do
he ⎫	he ⎫
she ⎬ do	she ⎬ does
it ⎭	it ⎭

PRESENT TENSE—PLURAL *to do*

Incorrect	Correct
we does	we do
you does	you do
they does	they do

PAST TENSE—SINGULAR *to do*

Incorrect	Correct
I done	I did
you done	you did
he } she } it done	he } she } it did

PAST TENSE—PLURAL *to do*

Incorrect	Correct
we done	we did
you done	you did
they done	they did

The main problem with *to do* is that it is used in informal speech differently than it is in writing. This common use makes it difficult to judge the correctness of *to do* by ear. All these sentences below, for example, are incorrect:

> He don't know what he's saying.

> I does what I have to.

> She done with him.

Here are the correct forms:

> He doesn't know what he's saying.

> I do what I have to.

> She is done with him.

If you are used to speaking the incorrect forms, don't trust your ear; instead, memorize the correct forms.

PRACTICING 9

Use the correct form of *to do* in the following sentences.

1. He _____ understand the subject.

2. She _____ carry on, _____ she?

3. _____ you know what the meeting is about?

4. How _____ you calculate that area?

5. Mary always _____ badly on the tennis court when she plays a match.

6. I _____ feel a sense of pride.

7. _____ she know about the sale?

8. Where _____ you find such good people?

9. _____ not speak to me that way!

10. It _____ not matter what you are talking about.

UNIT TEST

Fill in the blank with the correct form of the verb in parentheses.

1. Yesterday Julie (walk) _____ clear over to Jan's house.

2. My brother (be) _____ the best athlete in his class.

3. We are both guitarists, but he (be) _____ better than I (be) _____.

4. Felix (do) _____ take football too seriously.

5. Beverly still (smoke) _____ like a chimney.

6. Last year Stan (fish) _____ for a whole month in Montana.

7. She (hide) _____ every time I try to find her.

8. If you (be) _____ happy, that's all that matters.

9. The room (have) _____ a bad smell.

10. (Do) _____ she always do the best she can?

11. Doris and Jim (have) _____ too many burdens to carry.

12. The city (have) _____ to protect its citizens from fire hazards.

13. If she (do) _____ most of the work herself, it won't

be expensive.

14. The winner (take) _____ the entire purse.

15. The furniture (have) _____ to be waxed and polished.

UNIT TALKING ASSIGNMENT

Do this assignment with a classmate. The sentences that follow have singular subjects. Your classmate should read sentences 1–5 aloud. You will then write each sentence in the plural, making sure that the subject and verb agree. Read back the changed sentences and discuss them with your partner.

Then reverse your roles for sentences 6–10. Finally, with your partner check all of your written sentences to make sure that the subjects and verbs agree. (Note: sometimes there is more than one verb in the sentence.)

1. Every student needs a healthy breakfast.

_____

2. The train arrived from Philadelphia.

_____

3. He doesn't care about wealth.

_____

4. The woman pants because the hill is steep.

_____

5. A child forgets quickly.

_____

6. The gardener is delighted to see the sun is out.

_____

7. Does he live in town?

_____

8. I walk until I drop.

_____

9. That book has a torn cover.

_____

10. My wool sweater has no arms.

_____

UNIT WRITING ASSIGNMENT

Write a description of your childhood. Was it carefree? Happy? Lonely? Using brainstorming and freewriting, find a discussible point and support it with well-chosen details. When you have completed your writing, go over it to make sure that all of your verbs are correct.

Regular and Irregular Verbs

> **"The cat snuck into my bed."**
> **"He brung the book to school."**

Very early in life, our ear tells us that the past tense of a verb is usually signaled by *-ed* at the end. At first, we stubbornly apply this rule to every verb. It is not unusual to hear toddlers say, "I sitted on my chair," or "David hitted me with his cup." Later, we learn that the rule applies only to regular verbs, not to verbs that are irregular.

You can usually trust your ear with regular past tenses. However, with irregular past tenses, your ear cannot be trusted. The only solution is to memorize the irregular verbs.

In this unit you will learn when you can rely on your ear to select the correct verb tenses, and when you should lean more heavily on the formal rule.

Regular Verbs

Verbs are either regular or irregular. Regular verbs form the past tense by adding *-d* or *-ed*. They also form the past participle by adding *-d* or *-ed*. The past participle generally refers to actions in the distant, rather than the immediate, past. It requires a helping verb, either *have*, *has*, or *had*. Here are some examples of common regular verbs:

Present tense	Past tense	Past participle
charge	charged	have/has/had charged
cook	cooked	have/has/had cooked
pack	packed	have/has/had packed

Here are some examples of these words in sentences:

Past: She charged $7 per hour for painting the porch.

Past participle: She has charged less for simpler jobs.
She had charged Mr. Jones overtime.

Past: They packed the books yesterday.

Past participle: They have packed nearly everything now.
They had packed until nearly midnight.

Ear Alert

Don't let your ear fool you into dropping the -d or -ed endings of past tense verbs. Although this is a common mistake that we all occasionally make in everyday speech, you must not make it in your writing.

Dropped ending: We were suppose to meet her at the theater.

                       We were use to doing it that way.

Correct: We were suppose<u>d</u> to meet her at the theater.

                       We were use<u>d</u> to doing it that way.

In a Nutshell

- Regular verbs form the past tense by adding -*d* or -*ed*.

- Regular verbs form the past participle with the helping verb *to have* by adding -*d* or -*ed*.

- Don't be fooled by your ear into dropping the -*d* or -*ed*.

PRACTICING 1

Change the italicized regular verb in each sentence to the past participle. Remember to use *has*, *have*, or *had*. Write out the entire sentence.

Example: Fred *pumps* gas at an Arco station.

Fred has pumped gas at an Arco station.

1. I *part* my hair on the left side.

2. Jamie's father *looked* under the bed.

3. My favorite writer *appeared* on campus.

4. The private *salutes* the general.

5. We *vacation* in Santa Fe.

6. They *delivered* the furniture.

_____

7. The Zunis *live* in pueblos.

_____

8. Aunt Susan *talks* about getting a new job.

_____

9. The boys *mow* the lawn for a fee.

_____

10. You *helped* yourself.

_____

PRACTICING 2

The following sentences are adapted from a Southern woman's Civil War diary. Change the verb in parenthesis to its simple past tense.

1. Sherman's troops (march) past my window.

_____

2. Of course, we (expect) to sleep through the noise.

_____

3. They (surround) the campus with their sentries.

_____

4. The southern horizon (reflects) the glare of fire.

_____

5. I (imagine) night being turned into day by the blaze.

_____

6. The men (carry) buckets of water.

_____

7. The wounded from the hospital (help) as much as possible.

_____

8. The heat (forces) us away from the burning building.

_____

9. The flame (approach) from all sides.

_____

10. Snipers (fire) at the firefighters.

_____

11. The cannon (roar) with unspeakable might.

_____

12. The fire (wraps) the campus in the brightness of daylight.

_____

13. One soldier (apologizes) for the destruction.

_____

14. We (walk) away from him without speaking.

_____

15. We all (remember) that dreadful night.

_____

Omitting the helping verb in a past participle

In informal speech, it is common to drop the helping verb in a past participle—an act your ear might even excuse. But dropping the helping verb, whether your ear approves or not, is always wrong in writing. Here are some examples:

Dropped verb:	I been a team player.
Correct form:	I have been a team player.
Dropped verb:	I drawn the picture.
Correct form:	I have drawn the picture.
Dropped verb:	We driven around for ten minutes.
Correct form:	We had driven around for ten minutes.
Dropped verb:	Why Fred bought a white Honda?
Correct form:	Why has Fred bought a white Honda?

In a Nutshell

In writing, you must always include the helping verb of a past participle.

PRACTICING 3

Rewrite each sentence below in the line provided, inserting the helping verb where it belongs.

Example: Before the boss arrived, she cleaned her desk.

Before the boss arrived, she had cleaned her desk.

1. Most of the children written their parents letters from camp.

   _____

2. I been pretty poor all my life.

   _____

3. Many people seen cruelty and violence in their families.

   _____

4. Farmers in Fresno grown beautiful tomatoes.

   _____

5. He said he frozen the bananas to keep them from rotting.

   _____

6. Why you broken your promise?

   _____

7. Where you left your wallet?

   _____

8. He hidden the candy in the bottom drawer.

   _____

9. Lupe worn that coat since she was twelve.

   _____

10. The snow fallen early this winter.

   _____

PRACTICING 4

The paragraph that follows contains many errors in the use of past participles. First, underline each error; second, correct the errors.

What is a real American? Some people have claim that a real American is a person who is loyal, patriotic, and proud to live in the United States. Other people have suppose that a real American is someone who watches football on Monday nights and eats hot dogs. The definition of a real American changes constantly because different generations have experience different problems, such as war or depression. For instance, during the 1950s, when Senator Joseph McCarthy had made everyone paranoid about Communism, a "real American" was someone who was against Communism. Later, in the 1970s, a "real American" was someone who had battle the Vietnamese even though he might have believe that our efforts there were illogical and immoral.

During the later 1970s, a "real American" might have been someone who had purchase an American gas-guzzling car instead of a foreign economical car, just to show that he was supportive of the American economy. Today, the term "real American" is not easy to define because we have not experience a real war or crisis to pull us together. But this is what I think the term means: "A person who wants to change America for the better will fight to do so."

Irregular Verbs

Verbs are **irregular** if their past tense is not formed by adding *-d* or *-ed*. For example, if the rule for changing tenses were applied to *bring*, its past tense should be *bringed*, which it isn't—it's *brought*. *Bring* is therefore an irregular verb.

There is no single rule for forming the past tense of irregular verbs. You simply have to memorize the forms of those verbs that are irregular. In the past, students memorized these forms by chanting them. It is an old technique, but it works.

Below is a list of irregular verbs that many of us use practically every day. Remember, the past participle always requires the use of the helping verb *to have*.

Present	Past	Past participle
arise	arose	arisen
be	was	been
bear	bore	borne (not *born*)
become	became	become
begin	began	begun

Present	Past	Past participle
break	broke	broken
bring	brought (not *brung*)	brought
build	built	built
burst	burst (not *busted*)	burst
catch	caught	caught
buy	bought	bought
choose	chose	chosen
cling	clung	clung
come	came	come
dive	dove	dived
do	did (not *done*)	done
drag	dragged (not *drug*)	dragged
draw	drew	drawn
drink	drank	drunk
drive	drove	driven
fall	fell	fallen
eat	ate	eaten
feed	fed	fed
feel	felt	felt
fight	fought	fought
fly	flew	flown
forgive	forgave	forgiven
freeze	froze	frozen
get	got	gotten
go	went	gone
grow	grew	grown
hang (*clothes*)	hung	hung
hang (*execute*)	hanged	hanged
have	had	had
hold	held	held
hurt	hurt (not *hurted*)	hurt
know	knew	known
lead	led	led
lay	laid	laid
lie	lay	lain
lose	lost	lost
make	made	made
mean	meant	meant
meet	met	met
pay	paid	paid
put	put	put
read	read (pronounced like *red*)	read (pronounced like *red*)
ride	rode	ridden
ring	rrang	rung
rise	rose	risen

Present	Past	Past participle
run	ran	run
say	said	said
see	saw (not *seen*)	seen
seek	sought (not *seeked*)	sought
sell	sold	sold
set	set	set
shake	shook	shaken
shine	shone	shone
shrink	shrank	shrunk
sing	sang	sung
sink	sank	sunk
sleep	slept	slept
speak	spoke	spoken
spend	spent	spent
spin	spun	spun
spit	spat	spat
spring	sprang (not *sprung*)	sprung
stand	stood	stood
steal	stole	stolen
sting	stung	stung
stink	stank (not *stunk*)	stunk
strike	struck	struck
strive	strove	strove
swear	swore	sworn
swim	swam (not *swum*)	swum
swing	swung	swung
take	took	taken
teach	taught	taught
tear	tore	torn
tell	told	told
think	thought	thought
throw	threw	thrown
understand	understood	understood
wake	woke	woken
weave	wove	woven
wear	wore	worn
win	won	won
wring	wrung	wrung
write	wrote	written

If you don't know the past tense of an irregular verb, you can always look it up in a dictionary. For example, if you looked up the verb *give*, you would find its past tense listed as *gave* and its past participle as *given*. If the verb is regular, the dictionary will not give its past tense, which means that to form the past tense or past participle you simply add -d or -ed.

In a Nutshell

- An irregular verb is one whose past tense is not formed by adding -d or -ed.

- Irregular verbs must be memorized.

PRACTICING 5

Complete the following chart. If in doubt, refer to the list of irregular verbs on pages 80–82.

Present	Past	Past participle
1. drag	_____	_____
2. hurt	_____	_____
3. swim	_____	_____
4. spring	_____	_____
5. bring	_____	_____
6. see	_____	_____
7. freeze	_____	_____
8. ring	_____	_____
9. stink	_____	_____
10. choose	_____	_____

PRACTICING 6

In the following sentences, the past tense of the underlined verb is used incorrectly. Write the correct form of the verb in the space provided.

1. My friend <u>brung</u> me to school yesterday. _____

2. I <u>seen</u> him playing ball in the gym. _____

3. The cat <u>sprung</u> at the bird. _____

4. You know fully well what you <u>done</u>. _____

5. He <u>drug</u> the garbage can down the driveway. _____

6. I <u>drawed</u> a picture of the forest. _____

7. The pipe <u>busted</u> in the freezing weather. _____

8. You <u>stunk</u> after working in the garage. _____

9. Yesterday we <u>swum</u> in the city pool. _____

10. I <u>freezed</u> in the chilly water. _____

PRACTICING 7

Fill in the blank with the past tense of the verb in parentheses. Then, on the line below, write a sentence using the past participle of the verb. If you are in doubt, check the list of irregular verbs.

1. She (hang) _____ her underwear in a tree nearby.

   _____

   _____

2. The man (rise) _____ to allow the lady to be seated.

   _____

   _____

3. He (take) _____ down the kite from the tree.

   _____

   _____

4. Who (blow) _____ the whistle in the middle of the

   night?

   _____

   _____

5. Was it you who (drag) _____ the sack of potatoes

   into the living room?

   _____

   _____

6. She (swear) _____ eternal love to him.

   _____

   _____

7. The pigpens (stink) _____ really bad yesterday.

   _____

   _____

8. Today the birds fly; yesterday the birds (fly) _____.

_____

_____

9. Fred (tear) _____ a big hole in his pants.

_____

_____

10. Who (lead) _____ the opposition last year?

_____

_____

Problems with irregular verbs

Two problems are common with the everyday use of irregular verbs:

1. Using the simple past instead of the past participle.

Incorrect: He has ran in two marathons.

Correct: He has run in two marathons.

Incorrect: She has just wrote him a letter.

Correct: She has just written him a letter.

2. Using an incorrect form of the past or past participle.

Incorrect: She drug him along.

Correct: She dragged him along.

Incorrect: He has never wore that before.

Correct: He has never worn that before.

Beware of these two common errors.

PRACTICING 8

Some of the underlined past participles that follow are correct;
others are incorrect. If the participle is correct, place a *C* in the
blank; if it is incorrect, write the corrected participle in the blank.
If in doubt, check the list of irregular verbs.

Example: Most of the students should have <u>spoke</u> English. *spoken*

If you had <u>gone</u> to the store, we would have enough
milk for dinner. *C*

1. I have <u>ran</u> the Boston Marathon. _____

2. She has <u>swore</u> to bring up her grades. _____

3. One of the rugs she has <u>woven</u> is in the living room.

   _____

4. The soldiers had <u>dragged</u> the flag through mud and filth.

   _____

5. Before the party was over, all of the balloons had <u>bursted</u>.

   _____

6. Had I <u>knowed</u> then what I know now, I would be rich.

   _____

7. I have <u>swum</u> from here to the islands with no trouble.

   _____

8. I have <u>lead</u> in that competition all semester. _____

9. She had <u>took</u> much trouble to write a perfect essay.

   _____

10. Someone at the cafe had <u>stole</u> his wallet from the car.

    _____

11. She has not yet <u>paid</u> the rent for this month. _____

12. The taxi drivers <u>striked</u> the city at four this afternoon.

    _____

13. We <u>swinged</u> from the tree in the moonlight. _____

14. The had not <u>understanded</u> the problem. _____

15. She has <u>tore</u> a leaf from that book. _____

PRACTICING 9

Underline the correct form of the verb. Some sentences require the simple past tense, while others require the past participle form.

Example: They (fighted, <u>fought</u>) valiantly at the Battle of Bull Run.

1. We were surprised that the tomato vines had (grew, grown) so tall.

2. If the people had (forgiven, forgave) him, he probably would have survived.

3. Was it you who (brought, brung) the huge dog to church?

4. When was the last time you (driven, drove) the Hummer?

5. The chemistry professor (rode, ridden) in clear from Manchester.

6. Before he could stop her, she (spit, spat) on the floor.

7. For what reason had the townspeople (rang, rung) the bell?

8. Most of the sweaters had (shrunk, shrank) two sizes.

9. The little rowboat (sank, sunk) into the sea.

10. A large "B" had been (woven, wove) into the rug.

Problem Verbs

A few verbs seem to give the entire English-speaking world trouble. They are *lie/lay*, *sit/set*, and *rise/raise*.

Lie/lay

To lie means to rest in a horizontal position like a sleeper. *To lay* means to put or set down something as you might a book. To confuse matters further, the past tense of *lie* is *lay*.

Here are the principal parts of these two verbs.

Present	Past	Past participle
lie	lay	lain = to rest in a horizontal position like a sleeper
lay	laid	laid = to set down something, as you might do a book

Lie is always done *by* someone or something; *lay* is always done *to* someone or something. You lie down to take a nap, but you lay your glasses on the table. You lie in your bed, but you are laid to rest in your grave. Here are more examples:

To lie	To lay
I often lie on the floor to watch TV.	He lay the doll on the floor.
She is lying on the floor.	She is laying the doll on the floor.
Yesterday, I lay on the floor.	Yesterday she laid the doll on the floor.
I have lain on the floor.	I have laid the doll on the floor.

PRACTICING 10

Underline the correct verb.

1. "(Lie, Lay) down!" I shouted to my stubborn dog.

2. Tara had been (lying, laying) in bed daydreaming when the phone rang.

3. Within a month the contractor had (lain, laid) all the tile.

4. Yesterday Maxine (laid, lay) in bed with a cold.

5. All she does is (lie, lay) on the living room sofa watching soap operas.

6. Before they had (lain, laid) two miles of track, the mine exploded.

7. If you had (lain, laid) the ring in your jewelry box, it would not be lost.

8. Just to (lie, lay) on the cool, green grass and look at the clouds is heaven.

9. For two weeks Mary conscientiously (lay, laid) napkins on the table for every meal.

10. Yesterday Maxine (lay, laid) a blanket on her bed.

Sit/set

To sit means to rest on your bottom as you might do in a chair. *To set* means to place something somewhere. *To set* always requires an object except when it refers to the sun, which always sets but never sits.

Here are the principal parts of *sit* and *set*:

Present	Past	Past participle
sit	sat	sat = to rest on one's bottom
set	set	set = to place something somewhere

The basic difference is this: Someone or something *sits*; someone or something is *set*. So you *sit* on the floor, but you *set* the glass on the floor.

To sit	**To set**
The old man sits by the fire.	The man sets flowers on the table.
He is sitting by the fire.	He is setting the table.
All of us sat in stony silence.	Last year they set a record.
She has always sat in the back row.	Have you set your books down?

PRACTICING 11

Underline the correct verb.

1. I had (sat, set) the books on top of the piano.

2. For two hours, Marie (sat, set) on the bench and waited.

3. It felt to her as if she had (set, sat) there for two days.

4. Who is (setting, sitting) on his right?

5. (Sit, set) that box down this very moment!

6. We have (sat, set) around twiddling our thumbs long enough.

7. Had they told the truth instead of (setting, sitting) on it, they would have been better off.

8. (Sit, set) down and listen!

9. He (sat, set) the groceries on the sink.

10. Come and (sit, set) down next to me.

Rise/raise

To rise means to get up or move up on your own; *to raise* is to lift up someone or something or to cultivate or rear something.

Here are the principal parts of *rise* and *raise*:

Present	Past	Past participle
rise	rose	risen = to get up or move up on your own
raise	raised	raised = to lift up someone or something

You *rise* from a sitting position or *rise* to the top of your profession. You *raise* your arms or your voice; sometimes, you even *raise* Cain. You always *rise* to the occasion and doing so might get you a *raise* in pay.

Here are some other examples:

To rise	To raise
Let us rise and salute the flag.	Let us raise the flag on the pole.
She is rising to greet the man.	I am raising cattle.
The farmers have risen early.	The farmers have raised tons of corn.
The old men rose from the bench.	The old men raised their hands.

In a Nutshell

- *To lie* means to rest in a horizontal position; *to lay* means to put something down.

- *To sit* means to rest on your bottom; *to set* means to place something somewhere.

- *To rise* means to get up; *to raise* means to lift up something.

PRACTICING 12

Change the underlined word(s) by filling in *rise* or *raise* in the blanks provided. Do not change the tense of the original.

1. India <u>breeds</u> beautiful tigers. _____

2. What a thrill to see the sun <u>come up</u> over the hilltops!

   _____

3. The entire audience had <u>stood up</u> to applaud the rock band.

   _____

4. I <u>pulled up</u> the shades to see the tulips in the back yard.

   _____

5. The manager <u>has increased</u> Ellen's pay. _____

6. Lazarus is supposed to <u>have returned</u> from his grave.

   _____

7. He <u>increased</u> his grade point average this year.

   _____

8. She will <u>be equal</u> to the challenge of chemistry.

   _____

9. When she walks in, let's <u>get up</u> and applaud her eightieth

   birthday. _____

10. When taxes <u>become higher</u>, people demand a new presi-

    dent. _____

Lie/Lay, Sit/Set, Rise/Raise: Does It Really Matter?

If students don't ask the question, "Does it really matter if I say *lie* or *lay*?" they often think it. The answer is, yes, it does matter.

True, if you commanded *Lay down*! instead of *Lie down*! your dog would probably obey just as quickly. Many students might then wonder, "If I'm understood when I incorrectly say *lay* instead of *lie* or *lie* instead of *lay*, what does using the correct form matter?"

However, being understood is no substitute for being correct. Often, being correct is what makes you understandable.

Language does change, and as the years roll by we predict that one day *lie* and *lay* will have the same meaning in grammar books. Until that day comes, though, these differences do matter.

For example, you might scribble this memo to your boss: "Dear Boss, I lay the contract on your desk before I left." Upon reading it your boss might mutter, "No, you didn't. You laid it there. If you can't get that right, how can I trust you with this important contract? I'm giving the account to Nancy." In other words, these little differences are important because they matter to people.

Of course, they don't matter if you work for a dog.

UNIT TEST

Fill in the blanks with the correct past and past participle of the verb in the left column. Some of the verbs are regular, others are irregular.

Group A

Present	Past	Past participle
1. bring	_____	_____
2. drink	_____	_____
3. hunt	_____	_____
4. sing	_____	_____
5. speak	_____	_____
6. choose	_____	_____
7. lie	_____	_____
8. decide	_____	_____
9. ride	_____	_____
10. throw	_____	_____

Group B

Present	Past	Past participle
1. swim	_____	_____
2. wear	_____	_____
3. fear	_____	_____
4. raise	_____	_____
5. go	_____	_____
6. write	_____	_____
7. demand	_____	_____
8. study	_____	_____
9. forgive	_____	_____
10. eat	_____	_____

UNIT TALKING ASSIGNMENT

The following paragraph about the human desire for peace contains errors in the past participles of irregular verbs. First, correct the errors, then team up with a partner, exchange books, and check (correcting if necessary) each other's work. Discuss any mistakes, referring to the list of irregular verbs on pages 80–82 to settle any arguments.

The other day, while I drived along the freeway, I noticed a bumper sticker. It red, "Aim for peace." I thinked to myself, "Isn't peace what human beings all over the world want?" How many lives of every generation are drawed into the struggle for peace? Will peace be achieved only when millions of additional bodies are lain in unmarked graves? Martin Luther King, who lays buried in a Southern cemetery, killed by an assassin's bullet, tried to rise our consciousness for peace. His idea of peace didn't set well with the power structure of his day. Mohandas Gandhi also seeked peace for India. He, too, perished at the hand of an assassin who laid in wait for him. The wish for peace has obviously not just springed up. Human beings have always craved peace. Getting it, however, has not prove to be easy.

UNIT WRITING ASSIGNMENT

Below is a list of commonly seen bumper stickers. Choose one from the list and write about it. Or, choose a bumper sticker that you have on your own car or have seen and write about that. Pay particular attention to verb forms.

1. If you want peace, work for justice.
2. No phone. No job. No money. Retired.
3. The worst day fishing is better than the best day working.
4. I love N.Y.
5. Give a damn.
6. I brake for animals.
7. Baby on board.
8. Mother-in-law in trunk.
9. Because I'm your mother, that's why.
10. MADD—Mothers Against Drunk Drivers.

Subject-Verb Agreement

> "Fifi and Rex is well-trained dogs."

Subjects and verbs must agree in number: That is the one rule of subject-verb agreement. A singular subject always takes a singular verb; a plural subject always takes a plural verb. Most of the time this rule is plain and easy to follow, as shown in the following sentences:

> Jane loves John.

> The women love John.

Jane, a singular subject, takes the singular verb *loves*. *Women*, a plural subject, takes the plural verb *love*.

We are also likely to come across sentences like these:

> She don't watch much television.

> There is four reasons why I bought a Jeep.

She, a singular subject, is incorrectly paired with the plural verb *don't watch*. *Reasons*, a plural subject, is incorrectly paired with the singular verb *is*.

Although such mistakes are common in daily speech, writing demands a greater exactness. Subjects and verbs may disagree as they tumble out of the mouth, but on the page they must agree.

Subject-verb agreement errors are typically caused by some common grammatical situations. They are, in no particular order:

1. *Don't, was,* and *wasn't*:

   Incorrect: He don't care about me.

   Correct: He doesn't care about me.

   Incorrect: You was at the party.

   Correct: You were at the party.

2. *Each, every, either/or,* and *neither/nor*:

   Incorrect: Neither of us are going home.

   Correct: Neither of us is going home.

   Incorrect: Either of the cars are available.

   Correct: Either of the cars is available.

3. Prepositional phrase between a subject and verb:

    Incorrect: One of the three cousins are very smart.

    Correct: One of the three cousins is very smart.

4. Sentences beginning with *there/here*:

    Incorrect: There is a lot of chores to do.

    Correct: There are a lot of chores to do.

    Incorrect: Here is the correct answers.

    Correct: Here are the correct answers.

5. Questions:

    Incorrect: Where is the books?

    Correct: Where are the books?

6. Compound subjects joined by *and*, *or*, *either/or*, or *neither/nor*:

    Incorrect: The man and his son was smiling.

    Correct: The man and his son were smiling.

    Incorrect: The man or his son were smiling.

    Correct: The man or his son was smiling.

7. The indefinite pronouns *each*, *everyone*, *anybody*, *somebody*, and *nobody*:

    Incorrect: Everyone in the sociology class like the text.

    Correct: Everyone in the sociology class likes the text.

8. *Who*, *which*, and *that*:

    Incorrect: Richard is one of those students who works hard.

    Correct: Richard is one of those students who work hard.

We'll take up these situations one by one.

Do, Don't, Was, and Wasn't

Subject-verb agreement errors are often caused by the words *don't*, *was*, and *wasn't*. Here are the correct forms of *to do*:

Singular	**Plural**
I do	We do
You do	You do
He ⎫	They do
She ⎬ does	
It ⎭	

Among the most common subject-verb agreement errors made is the use of *he* or *she* with *do* instead of the correct *does*:

Incorrect: He do his job quite well.

Correct: He does his job quite well.

This error occurs second only to the incorrect use of *don't* with a singular subject:

Incorrect: She don't know what she's talking about.

Correct: She doesn't know what she's talking about.

Was and *wasn't* are also often involved in many subject-verb agreement errors. Here are the correct forms:

Singular	**Plural**
I was	We were
You were	You were
He ⎫	They were
she ⎬ was	
it ⎭	

Here are some examples of errors commonly made with this verb:

Incorrect: You was at the party.

Correct: You were at the party.

Incorrect: You was so nice to me when I was sick.

Correct: You were so nice to me when I was sick.

In a Nutshell

Do, *don't*, *was*, and *wasn't* often cause subject-verb agreement errors. Always check to be sure you've used them correctly.

PRACTICING 1

Underline the correct form of the verb in parentheses.

Example: Many of us (was, <u>were</u>) happy when it rained.

1. That green chair (doesn't, don't) match the blue table.

2. (Wasn't, weren't) you at home when he arrived?

3. The end (doesn't, don't) always justify the means.

4. Jimmy and Frank (was, were) both great swimmers.

5. She (don't, doesn't) ever deliver what she promises.

6. (Was, were) those the only letters you wrote?

7. (Doesn't, don't) it matter to you that you hurt her feelings?

8. Many of the cows (were, was) hungry and diseased.

9. There (are, is) many days when I want to stay home.

10. Both the sergeant and the corporal (was, were) nice people.

Each, Every, Either/Or, and Neither/Nor

Among some troublesome subjects are the words *each*, *every*, *either*, *either/or*, *neither*, and *neither/nor*. All take a singular verb. Here are some examples:

Each hat, coat, and umbrella was (not <u>were</u>) assigned a number.

Every piano and violin is (not <u>are</u>) being used for the performance.

Neither of the students works (not <u>work</u>) very hard.

Either of the cars is (not <u>are</u>) a bargain.

Don't be confused by the prepositional phrase—for example, *of the cars*—that usually follows *each*, *every*, *either*, or *neither*. Cross it out, as we suggested in Unit 1, and the verb choice will be clear.

Either/or and *neither/nor* are also troublesome. Here are some examples:

| **Incorrect:** | Neither the principal nor the guidance counselor know me by name. |
| **Correct:** | Neither the principal nor the guidance counselor knows me by name. |

| **Incorrect:** | Neither the secretary nor the president were to blame. |
| **Correct:** | Neither the secretary nor the president was to blame. |

If one subject joined by *either/or* or *neither/nor* is singular and one is plural, the verb should agree with the nearer subject.

| **Incorrect:** | Either the rats or the raccoon were here. |
| **Correct:** | Either the rats or the raccoon was here. |

    Incorrect: Either one grown-up or two youngsters has to carry the chair.

    Correct: Either one grown-up or two youngsters have to carry the chair.

In a Nutshell

Each, *every*, *either/or*, and *neither/nor* take singular verbs except when they join two subjects, one singular and one plural, in which case the verb agrees with the nearer subject.

PRACTICING 2

In the following sentences, underline the correct form of the verb in parentheses.

Example: Neither of the boats (are, <u>is</u>) sinking.

1. Each of the girls (has, have) a purple hat.

2. Neither of the books (is, are) written in fine print.

3. Either of them (are, is) suitable for the test.

4. Every house within two blocks (is, are) rented.

5. Each hat and umbrella (was, were) assigned a number.

6. Every car and truck (are, is) available for leasing.

7. Each of the thousand applicants (take, takes) a number.

8. Neither of the boys (understands, understand) the explanation.

9. Either crisis (is, are) enough for now.

10. Every goose and duck (is, are) playing in the pond.

Phrases Between a Subject and Its Verb

A prepositional phrase that comes between a subject and verb can cause an agreement error. Here is a list of common prepositions:

about	after	among	before
above	against	around	behind
across	along	at	below

beneath	for	on	toward
beside	from	out	under
besides	in	outside	underneath
between	inside	over	until
beyond	into	past	up
by	like	since	upon
despite	near	throughout	with
down	of	through	within
during	off	to	without
except			

Here is a typical agreement error caused by a prepositional phrase coming between a subject and verb:

One of the blue cars were out of gas.

The prepositional phrase *of the blue cars* comes between the subject *one* and the verb *were*. The subject, though, is still *one*, and *one* is always singular. Cross out the prepositional phrase and the subject is immediately clear:

One ~~of the blue cars~~ was out of gas.

In a Nutshell

An agreement error can be caused by a prepositional phrase that comes between a subject and its verb.

PRACTICING 3

In the sentences that follow, cross out all prepositional phrases. Circle the subjects and underline the correct forms of the verbs in parentheses.

1. The houses at the end of our block (is, are) old.

2. The stairs behind the library (is, are) very steep.

3. That box of clothes and books (go, goes) to the garage sale.

4. An analysis of the tissues (indicates, indicate) that disease is present.

5. Five stores in the old alley (shows, show) signs of damage.

6. A group of Hollywood stars (is, are) forming their own movie studio.

7. This comment about The Rolling Stones (explains, explain) their songs.

8. At Ralph's a package of dried bananas (sells, sell) for less.

9. A quilt of little blue patches (hangs, hang) on the wall.

10. The diamonds scattered on the counter (looks, look) unreal.

Sentences Beginning with There/Here

Subject-verb agreement errors can easily occur in sentences that begin with *there is*, *there are*, *here is*, and *here are*. Here are some examples:

Incorrect: There was two strangers dressed in black.
Correct: There were two strangers dressed in black.

Incorrect: Here is the pencils you asked me to buy.
Correct: Here are the pencils you asked me to buy.

In these examples, the writer is confused by *there* or *here*, which strikes the ear as singular. However, neither *here* nor *there* is the subject of the sentence. If you're confused by such sentences, reword them to make the subject come before the verb and the mistake will quickly become visible:

Two strangers dressed in black were there.

The pencils you asked me to buy are here.

Indeed, many sentences beginning with *there* or *here* can be made crisper and better if they are reworded to avoid such dead openings. Here is an example:

Original: There are many children who go to bed hungry.
Rewrite: Many children go to bed hungry.

The *there is* or *there are* is often unnecessary.

In a Nutshell

Watch out for subject-verb agreement errors in sentences that begin with *there* or *here*. To check the agreement of such a sentence, reword it to place the subject first.

PRACTICING 4

Underline the correct form of the verb in parentheses. Circle the subject.

1. There (is, are) the snowcapped mountains.

2. There (was, were) three papers about cats.

3. Here (is, are) a map of India.

4. There (is, are) moments in my life when I would like to be a hermit.

5. Here (is, are) the towels you borrowed.

6. There (is, are) three dresses hanging in the closet.

7. There (was, were) two shacks between the house and the mansion.

8. There (was, were) many Italian songs sung that night.

9. There (was, were) big iron pots boiling and bubbling on the stove.

10. Here (is, are) the autographs you wanted.

PRACTICING 5

Rewrite each sentence below to avoid the *there* or *here* beginning and to make the writing crisper.

1. There is a mountain of laundry to be washed.

   _____

2. Here are the two diaries for you to read and enjoy.

   _____

3. There are certain bandplayers who would prefer to play golf than perform.

   _____

4. Here is the computer expert who promised to install your hardware.

   _____

5. There are details that need to be added to the paragraph.

Questions

Most sentences that we write or speak are statements, such as these:

> The newspaper is here.

> The toast is brown.

> The coffee is burned.

In these, and in most statements, because the subject comes before the verb, it is easy to spot an agreement error.

However, when we ask a question, the verb typically comes before the subject:

> Where is the newspaper?

> What color is the toast?

> What happened to the coffee?

With the subject now following the verb, it is easy to make an agreement error:

> Where is John and Mary sitting?

To use the plural verb *are* correctly requires a speaker or writer to know that a plural subject—*John and Mary*—lies ahead. If you're in doubt about the agreement between subject and verb in a question, simply reword it as a statement. For example, we have:

> John and Mary (is/are) sitting here.

It is now evident that the plural *are* is the correct verb since *John and Mary* refer to two people.

In a Nutshell

To check subject-verb agreement in a question, simply reword it as a statement.

PRACTICING 6

Underline the correct form of the verb in parentheses in the following questions.

1. What (is, are) the names of the players?

2. Where on earth (do, does) such people live?

3. Where (is, are) Daddy's gloves?

4. How many attorneys (do, does) the accused have?

5. What (has, have) the people done about it?

6. What (is, are) Donna's favorite subjects?

7. Who (is, are) those strangers coming up the walkway?

8. (Have, has) the tenants complained to the landlord?

9. What (has, have) they said about me?

10. After all, what (do, does) they know?

Compound Subjects Joined by And, Or, Either/Or, or Neither/Nor

The sentence that occasionally gives writers trouble is one that looks like this:

SINGULAR NOUN + AND + SINGULAR NOUN

Here are some examples:

The man and the woman was there.

The house and the car is mine.

Time and energy makes a difference.

In all these sentences, the writer was fooled by what seemed to be a singular subject. However, just as one plus one makes two, one singular subject plus another singular subject joined by *and* always makes a subject plural. The sentences should therefore read:

The man and the woman <u>were</u> there.

The house and the car <u>are</u> mine.

Time and energy <u>make</u> a difference.

Just remember that one plus one makes two, and two is plural.

Another test is to substitute a suitable pronoun for the double subject. For example, the sentence,

>   The man and the woman was there.

becomes

>   They was there.

which should strike your ear as wrong. The correct sentence is therefore

>   They were here.

or

>   The man and woman were there.

Although two singular subjects joined by *and* always take a plural verb, two singular subjects joined by *or* require a singular verb:

>   Burt and Tom are on the team.

but

>   Burt or Tom is on the team.

>   Joan and Linda are coming.

but

>   Joan or Linda is coming.

Of course, two plural nouns joined by *or* take a plural verb:

>   Usually, captains or co-captains are elected.

What happens when a sentence has two subjects, one singular and one plural, joined by *or*? In that case, the verb agrees with the nearer subject:

>   The co-captains or the coach <u>is</u> calling a meeting.

but

>   The coach or the co-captains <u>are</u> calling a meeting.

As we saw earlier in the chapter, the same rule applies with two subjects joined by *either/or* and *neither/nor*: The verb agrees with the nearer subject:

>   Either the co-captains or the coach <u>is</u> calling a meeting.

but

>   Either the coach or the co-captains <u>are</u> calling a meeting.

In a Nutshell

- Two singular subjects joined by *and* are plural.

- Two singular subjects joined by *or*, *either or*, or *neither/nor* are singular.

- If a singular and plural subject are joined by *or*, *either/or*, or *neither/nor*, the verb agrees with the closer subject.

PRACTICING 7

Complete the following sentences using a correct singular or plural verb form, followed by a prepositional phrase.

Example: Juan or Frederico always *takes out the garbage.*

1. Neither the teacher nor the students _____

2. Either your or I _____

3. Fighting or screaming _____

4. Neither money nor power _____

5. Neither Pat nor I _____

6. Avocado or papaya _____

7. Two apples or one orange _____

8. Neither his lovers nor his wife _____

9. Neither that vase nor those plates _____

10. Either his favorite books or his favorite bed _____

PRACTICING 8

In the following sentences, underline the correct form of the verb in parentheses.

1. His bristling eyebrows and large frown (scare, scares) children.

2. Love and marriage (goes, go) together like a horse and carriage.

3. A fool and his money (is, are) soon parted.

4. Los Angeles and Long Beach (is, are) good places to live.

5. Soup and salad (is, are) a favorite meal of many weight-conscious people.

6. Arthritis and the pains of old age (affect, affects) many older people.

7. London and Paris (is, are) attractive to tourists.

8. The gorilla and chimpanzee (was, were) observed crossing the grassy ridge.

9. My mother and father (inspires, inspire) me to achieve.

10. Undeserved praise and lies (amounts, amount) to the same thing.

The Indefinite Pronouns, Everyone, Anyone, Somebody, and Nobody

Indefinite pronouns are so called because they refer to no specific—or definite—person. The following indefinite pronouns always take a singular verb:

another	everything
anybody	nobody
anything	no one
everybody	nothing
everyone	one
anyone	somebody

Here are some examples:

Everybody has (not <u>have</u>) the right to freedom of speech.

Everyone tells (not <u>tell</u>) a different story.

Nobody knows (not <u>know</u>) the truth better than I do.

Another says (not <u>say</u>) something else.

In a Nutshell

Indefinite pronouns such as *everyone*, *everything*, *everybody*, and *nobody* take singular verbs.

PRACTICING 9

Underline the correct form of the verb in parentheses.

1. Everyone (has, have) an opinion.

2. Most of the clouds (is, are) below the mountain range.

3. Everybody (loves, love) a beautiful sunset.

4. No one (refuses, refuse) to paint their houses.

5. None of the chocolate (is, are) melted.

6. Anybody who is somebody (knows, know) the mayor personally.

7. One of the actors (wears, wear) a false nose.

8. Somebody (know, knows) who ate my porridge.

9. Everything you say (is, are) a lie.

10. Nobody (knows, know) my name.

Who, Which, and That

Who, *which*, and *that* are often used to replace nouns in dependent clauses. When they are so used, they should agree with the closest preceding noun. Consider this example:

Incorrect: John is among the men who thinks we have a problem.

Correct: John is among the men who think we have a problem.

The closest noun that went before *who* is not *John* but *men*. It is *men* that therefore determines the form of the verb. In fact, the sentence is a blend of two smaller sentences:

John is among the men. The men think we have a problem.

The *who* stands for *men* not for *John*. If you have trouble with this rule, split the sentence into two smaller sentences, and the subject will become clear.

Here are other examples:

Jeff or Joe is one of those who are going to Tibet.

Those, not *Jeff* or *Joe*, is the closest noun before *who*.

Among our daily plagues and troubles is a fly that bites.

Fly, not *plagues* or *troubles*, is the closest noun before *that*.

In a Nutshell

Who, *which*, and *that* used in dependent clauses must agree with the closest preceding noun.

PRACTICING 10

Circle the closest noun preceding *who*, *which*, or *that* in the following sentences. Then underline the correct form of the verb in parentheses.

1. A coach who (allow, allows) personal attacks on an opposing player teaches bad sportsmanship.

2. Bob is one of the players who (score, scores) regularly.

3. Peter is the only student who (qualify, qualifies) for advanced math.

4. Marie is one of the dancers who (hopes, hope) to go to New York.

5. These two movies, which (contains, contain) pointless violence, should not win Oscars.

6. Betty is among the students who (is, are) dissatisfied.

7. The questions that (has, have) come in has to do with cost and color.

8. These herb tablets, which (look, looks) harmless, can cause an upset stomach.

9. The big, billowy clouds that (fill, fills) the sky make me feel like singing.

10. He is one of those who (object, objects) to the proposal.

UNIT TEST

Use your imagination to complete the following sentences, making verb and subject agree.

1. One of the dogs that _____

2. Either of the desks _____

3. There is _____

4. The amount of work _____

5. Nobody in this town ever _____

_____

6. Stinginess, among other faults, _____

_____

7. At the edge of town was _____

8. Not only the assistants but the manager _____

_____

9. Talent and hard work _____

10. The paper and the ribbon on this gift package _____

_____

11. Neither his beloved cat nor all four dogs _____

_____

12. Pete by himself or the committee members _____

_____

13. Both the gorgeous pink roses and the silver ribbon _____

_____

14. There are _____

15. Here is _____

UNIT TALKING ASSIGNMENT

A. The following paragraph contains errors in subject-verb agreement. Make all the required corrections. Then exchange papers with a partner and discuss your answers.

Old age and youth is different. Whereas children move from childhood to adulthood, what role does senior citizens progress to? In this country there is only two generations, parents and children. A grandmother often do not play an essential role in our society. Instead, she spend her life feeling unnecessary. No wonder so few of my friends' parents wants to retire, but keep on working past the age of sixty-five. They feel that if they gives up working, they will be ignored and forgotten. Both our young people and the state has a responsibility to help the aged, whose taxes kept our economy stable. That does not mean that we should spoil senior citizens by letting them vegetate in comfort. Helping them and caring for them means finding creative jobs which appeals to what the elderly can do. Old people needs solid roles that makes them feel important. To feel useful and to engage in some significant activity gives older people a sense of self-worth.

B. Choose a partner, and talk out a paragraph about a person you admire. This person might be one of the following:

1. A relative, family friend, neighbor, teacher, or coach
2. A political figure
3. A sports personality
4. An entertainer
5. Someone you've read about

UNIT WRITING ASSIGNMENT

Write about the person you described in the Unit Talking Assignment above.

Problems with Verbs

> **"Mom fed me an egg, then just ignores me."**
> **"I would of gone if invited."**
> **"A good time was had by all."**

If English is a car, then the verb is its engine. Like the engine of a real car, the verb is the part of speech that is most likely to cause problems. In this unit we will cover some common problems with verbs. Specifically, we'll deal with the following:

- Shifts in tense

- Using *would of, could of*, or *should of* instead of *would have, could have*, or *should have*

- Double negatives

- Active and passive voice

Shifts in Tense

If you begin a sentence in the present tense, you must end it in the present tense. If you begin in the past tense, you must end in the past tense. For example, look at this sentence:

> Mom fed me an egg, then just ignores me.

The problem with the sentence is that it begins with a verb in the past tense and ends with a verb in the present tense. Mom is made into a time-traveler—hopping from the past to the present in one breath. To be correct the sentence must read:

Mom fed me an egg and then just   **(all past tense)**
ignored me.

or

Mom feeds me an egg and then just   **(all present tense)**
ignores me.

Your tense use must be consistent. If there is no logical reason for jumping from present to past or past to present, you must not do so.

Ear Alert

Yet, because we mix up our verb tenses all the time in everyday speech, your ear might mislead you into making the same mistake in writing. Be alert to this possible error. Make sure your verbs in a written sentence all use the same tense.

In a Nutshell

Verbs in the same sentence must all be in the same tense.

PRACTICING 1

Correct the shifts in verb tense in these sentences.

1. The thief stole all four wheels and leaves the car hulk on the sidewalk.

   _____

2. When I told her the package had arrived, she simply shrugs.

   _____

3. The doctor asks me lots of questions and then gave me a shot of penicillin.

   _____

4. When they demanded to see the manager, a secretary tells them to wait.

   _____

5. I had just surfed a wave when an unexpected wave hits me from the back.

   _____

6. The grizzly leaned over and scoops a salmon from the stream.

   _____

7. On his birthday, Bernie bought a lottery ticket and wins.

   _____

8. When the bell rings, all of the children assembled in the auditorium.

   _____

9. My mother recites the poem "Bobby Shaftoe," and we broke up with laughter.

_____

10. She ran past me and yells, "Hurry up!"

_____

11. She sees the cereal and shouted, "I want that, Mommy!"

_____

12. For as long as he lived, he believes he was right.

_____

13. He unfurled the sail and starts up the motor.

_____

14. My boy loved our rowboat and wants to take it out on the lake.

_____

15. The bass were biting well so we do not stop fishing.

_____

PRACTICING 2

Complete the sentences below, using the correct verb tense.

Example: Her mother scolded her and _made her realize her mistake._

1. I came, I saw, and I _____

2. The diver checks his oxygen and then _____

_____

3. Once the emergency team had her on her back, they _____

_____

4. When Dad had his coffee, Marie _____

5. The violins tune, the singers hum, and the conductor _____

_____

Would Have, Could Have, or Should Have

Although in speech _would have_ often sounds like _would of, would of, could of,_ or _should of_ are actually nothing more than mispronunciations. You should never use _would of, could of,_ or _should of_ in your writing.

PRACTICING 3

Correct the use of *would of, could of,* or *should of* in the sentences below.

1. I would of come if you had told me.

_____

2. Should we of accompanied her to the bridge?

_____

3. For the right price, she could of bought the car.

_____

4. I know I should of burned that letter.

_____

5. If he would of reported the crime, the police would of come.

_____

6. She never should of promised to move to Connecticut.

_____

7. She could of been my best friend in a different school.

_____

8. You would of liked Joe, my best friend.

_____

9. Everyone should of shared in the expense.

_____

10. If we would of been more patient, Mary would of stayed in college.

_____

Double Negatives

Use only one negative for each idea. Do not use a negative qualifier (*no, not,* or *never*) with a negative verb or with the adverbs *hardly* or *scarcely*.

Incorrect: She didn't buy no onions.
Correct: She didn't buy any onions.

Incorrect: I can't hardly wait for spring break.
Correct: I can hardly wait for spring break.

Incorrect: John wouldn't scarcely give her the time of day.
Correct: John would scarcely give her the time of day.

Incorrect: The boys hadn't found no apples.
Correct: The boys hadn't found any apples.

PRACTICING 4

Rewrite each sentence that follows to correct the double negative.

1. Nobody knew nothing about the theft.

_____

2. We never play no card games.

_____

3. Tom can't hardly wait for the peaches to ripen.

_____

4. She never ordered no donuts.

_____

5. All of us wouldn't scarcely mention the picnic to her.

_____

6. The storage area didn't contain no usable bicycles.

_____

7. Didn't the police ask you no questions?

_____

8. In second grade I hardly spoke no English.

_____

9. Although they looked at us, they didn't give us no trouble.

_____

10. The judges wouldn't speak no score aloud.

_____

Active and Passive Voice

English has two voices: the active and the passive voice. The **active voice** stresses who did an act. The **passive voice** stresses to whom or to what an act was done. Most of us usually speak in the active voice because it is simpler and more direct.

Active voice: The students greeted the professor.
Passive voice: The professor was greeted by the students.

Because it hides the doer, the passive voice is often preferred by writers who wish to avoid naming names. Here is a case in point:

> The oak trees were ordered to be bulldozed to make room for a high-rise office complex.

Who gave this order? The active voice would have told us:

> Commissioner Smith ordered the oak trees to be bulldozed to make room for a high-rise office complex.

In writing you should mainly use the active voice. It is livelier, stronger, and more like everyday talk than the passive voice. The passive voice is occasionally used in scientific reporting, where what was done is more important than which researcher did it:

> The bacteria were isolated for further study.

The passive voice is also occasionally used in instances where an act is more important than its cause:

> The village was destroyed by a terrible flood.

The important fact here is the destruction of the village. That it was destroyed by a flood is secondary.

In a Nutshell

Write mainly in the active voice, which is livelier and stronger than the passive voice.

PRACTICING 5

Read the paired sentences aloud and place an *A* in the blank beside the sentences in the active voice.

Example: __A__   a. The children turned on the lights.

            _____   b. The lights were turned on by the children.

1. _____ **a.** The vacation was announced by the teacher.

   _____ **b.** The teacher announced the vacation.

2. _____ **a.** Students are hurt by the battle for grades.

_____ **b.** The battle for grades hurts students.

3. _____ **a.** Some months Fred owes more money than he makes.

_____ **b.** Some months more money is owed by Fred than he makes.

4. _____ **a.** The church deceived its members.

_____ **b.** The members were deceived by the church.

5. _____ **a.** The renters were told to evacuate the building.

_____ **b.** The police told the renters to evacuate the building.

PRACTICING 6

Rewrite the sentences below to change from the passive to the active voice.

Example: The chili was burned by the cook.

The cook burned the chili.

1. The point was made by the field-goal kicker.

_____

2. The plane was struck by the bird.

_____

3. The stamps were bought by Harry and the letters were mailed by Mary.

_____

4. The bear was tracked by the hunting dogs.

_____

5. The contract was signed last week by Mr. Hammer.

_____

6. The proposition was opposed by a vocal minority of students.

_____

7. Weightlifting is done by the students.

_____

8. The popcorn was popped by the fraternity member.

_____

9. The roof was blown off by the explosion.

_____

10. A deal was struck by the truck drivers.

_____

11. A diet was begun by the gymnast.

_____

12. The lopsided houses were built by the contractor.

_____

13. Tenses in English are used by all speakers.

_____

14. The beanstalk is cut down by Jack.

_____

15. Tasteless jokes were made by the unfunny comedian.

_____

UNIT TEST

Rewrite each sentence, correcting any mistakes.

1. She could of slept all day.

_____

2. They don't have no time for us.

_____

3. She scrambled to her feet and looks him in the eye.

_____

4. All of us should of thanked our guide.

_____

5. A bone was given to the dog by Mark.

_____

6. I never promised you nothing whatsoever.

_____

7. We don't never have any fun.

_____

8. My dad don't never play with me.

_____

9. Don't feed me no garbage today.

_____

10. Fran don't never open her book to study.

_____

UNIT TALKING ASSIGNMENT

A. The following paragraph contains shifts in verb tense, double negatives, and incorrect use of would have, could have, and should have. It also uses the passive voice when the active would be more effective. Rewrite the paragraph making all required corrections. Exchange papers with a partner, then discuss your answers and any points of disagreement.

I arrived in Paris and quickly settle into a decent youth hostel. I realize that I was running out of money. "If only I would of spent less money in England," I thought regretfully. My next thought was, "I'd better get a job." The problem was that I didn't have no work permit. I didn't speak French very well. No one wanted to hire me since work could not be performed by me legally. My concern would of turned into desperation if I had not met a friend at the post office who suggests that I try the American Church situated along the Seine River. The church had posted several advertisements for nannies. Before long, I land a job, but it does not last long because my position was temporary. I could have born this hardship if I would of received some decent meals. However, the French family I work for ate French bread, cheese, and cabbage day in and day out. So I quit. A few days later, a nanny job was found by me for a four-year-old girl who lived near Versailles. The job was worthwhile because the little girl has such a sweet temperament. My six months in Paris helped me to be independent both emotionally and financially. It is a great experience.

B. Discuss with your partner a job you have or once had. Talk out a paragraph on this topic.

UNIT WRITING ASSIGNMENT

Write about a job you have or once had, based on your discussion in the Unit Talking Assignment above.

Using Pronouns Correctly

> **"Maggie's sister encouraged her to wear her miniskirt."**

If writing were baseball, the pronoun would be a relief pitcher whose job is temporarily to relieve nouns, who are the starters. In both speech and writing, the **pronoun** is a word used in place of a noun.

Here is a paragraph that might be written in a world without pronouns:

> My favorite aunt is my Aunt Ida. Aunt Ida is my mother's sister. Aunt Ida loves to read. Aunt Ida reads everything, especially romance novels. Aunt Ida's house is crammed full of books. One room, which Aunt Ida calls Aunt Ida's library, is filled to the brim with books Aunt Ida has read. Aunt Ida not only reads many books, but Aunt Ida also saves every book Aunt Ida has read. Why? Because, Aunt Ida says, Aunt Ida loves rereading old books Aunt Ida has already read.

This paragraph is repetitious and stiff because it uses no pronouns. Adding a few pronouns makes the writing livelier and more natural:

> My favorite aunt is my Aunt Ida. She is my mother's sister. Aunt Ida loves to read. She reads everything, especially romance novels. Her house is crammed full of books. One room, which she calls her library, is filled to the brim with books she has read. Aunt Ida not only reads many books, but she also saves every book she has read. Why? Because, Aunt Ida says, she loves rereading old books she has already read.

All speakers use pronouns by ear, often without even thinking. Although our ear gets them right for the most part, because pronoun use in speech is more informal than in writing, we can't rely on our ear alone. We also need to learn the formal rules of pronoun use. That is what this unit covers.

Here are some common problems associated with pronouns in both speaking and writing:

- Referent problems

- Agreement problems

- Shifting point of view

We'll take up these problems in order.

Referent Problems

The **referent** of a pronoun is the noun it replaces. Consider this sentence:

John may be shy, but he loves to go to parties.

The pronoun is *he*; its referent—the word it refers to—is *John*.

Most of the time, the referent of a pronoun is perfectly clear from the context of a sentence. Sometimes, however, it isn't. Sometimes a referent is either unclear or altogether missing.

Unclear referents

Here are some examples of unclear referents:

Sheila drove Sylvia and her mother to the airport.

Harriett asked Janet if she needed an umbrella.

In the above sentences, the referents of the pronouns are unclear. We do not know whether Sheila drove her mother or Sylvia's mother to the airport, or whether it is Harriet or Janet who needs an umbrella. Here are the same sentences rewritten to avoid the unclear referent:

Sheila drove Sylvia and Sylvia's mother to the airport.

or

Sheila drove her mother and Sylvia to the airport.

Harriett asked Janet if Janet needed an umbrella.

or

Harriett asked Janet if she, Harriett, needed an umbrella.

Sometimes the unclear referent is not a person, but an action, feeling, or episode.

Unclear: Not only was the fish old, but Sally paid too much, which really made her mad.

Was Sally angry because the fish was old, because she overpaid, or both?

Clear: Not only was the fish old, but Sally paid too much, both of which made her mad.

Unclear: The Coast Guard located the missing boat within an hour and rescued the boys, who said they were not frightened by the experience. This amazed their parents.

What does *this* refer to? We do not know. It could refer either to the boy's rescue, their supposed lack of fear, or both.

> **Clear:**   The Coast Guard located the missing boat
>   within three hours and rescued the boys, who
>   said they were not frightened by the experience.
>   The parents were amazed by the Coast's Guard's
>   quick response.

Now we know exactly what the writer means. Note that to get around an unclear referent, you may need to rewrite the sentence.
Here is yet another example of a pronoun with an unclear referent:

> **Unclear:**   Sharon arrived late and quietly took a seat
>   in the back row. Everyone agreed that was very
>   unlike her.

What is the referent for *that*? The referent could be that *she arrived late* or that *she quietly took a seat in the back row*.

> **Clear:**   Sharon arrived late, which was very unlike her, and
>   quietly took a seat in the back row.

In the back-and-forth of daily talk, unclear referents are cleared up easily. The listener blurts out, "Who?" and gets a clarifying answer. However, in writing we get no chance to ask the writer *who*? If a pronoun does not have a clear referent, you risk confusing your reader.

In a Nutshell

Every pronoun must have a clear referent.

PRACTICING 1

Rewrite the following sentences so that the pronouns clearly refer to only one referent.

1. Mathilda held a Coke in one hand and water in the other, drinking it while she spoke.

_____

_____

2. Betty baked cookies for Caroline, which she thought was a nice gesture.

_____

_____

3. We took the curtains off the windows and cleaned them.

_____

_____

4. Bob and Harry started a business that went bankrupt because he always spent money before it was made.

_____

_____

5. Mary should help Joan, but she should help herself first.

_____

_____

6. My brother was best friends with our neighbor's son until he left for college.

_____

_____

7. Maggie's sister encouraged her to wear her miniskirt.

_____

_____

8. Professor Jones implied to Jack that he was far too liberal for his own good.

_____

_____

9. Charlie told Julio that he had been rude.

_____

_____

10. John screwed up his courage and told his friend that he owed him money.

_____

_____

Missing referents

In both speech and writing, we often use pronouns with missing referents. This is especially true of the pronouns *which*, *this*, *that*, *they*, and *it*. Here is an example:

Even though my mother is a marathon runner, I have no interest in it.

What is the *it*? We have a fuzzy idea that by *it*, the writer means *running*, but the word *running* does not appear in the sentence.

Usually, the best way to rewrite such a sentence is to omit the pronoun and provide the missing noun.

> Even though my mother is a marathon runner, I have no interest in running.

The missing referent problem is especially common with the pronouns *which*, *this*, and *that*. The best fix for such absent referents is simply to supply the noun. Here are some examples:

Missing: At the Emergency Room, they said Mara had broken her ankle.

Who is this mysterious *they* in the sentence?

Clear: At the Emergency Room, the doctor said Mara had broken her ankle.

Incorrect: It says to print your name under your signature.

Correct: The directions say to print your name under your signature.

Now we know the identity of the unnamed *it*.

The requirement that every pronoun have a specific and clear referent is not simply a picky rule. In everyday talk we do not observe such exactness in pronoun use because we can always ask "What?" and get an answer. In writing, though, you have no second chance. Every pronoun must therefore have a specific referent.

In a Nutshell

Be alert to the chance of a missing referent when using the pronouns *which*, *this*, *that*, *they*, and *it*.

PRACTICING 2

Rewrite the following sentences to clarify the pronoun reference.

1. We were standing in line when they informed us that the show was sold out.

_____

_____

2. In the directions, it says to add one cup of flour.

_____

_____

3. My sister refused to go to college because she felt they required too much math for graduation.

_____

_____

4. He destroyed the garden and ruined the driveway, which saddened my mother.

_____

_____

5. It says to change the oil every 3 months or 3,000 miles.

_____

_____

6. Most of my classmates write poems, but I have no talent for it.

_____

_____

7. I deposited the money in my bank, but they haven't posted the correct balance.

_____

_____

8. Mary bragged about her dancing ability although she had never been one.

_____

_____

9. We ordered a large pizza, but they delivered a medium.

_____

_____

10. Claire said they advised her to have a perm.

_____

_____

Agreement Problems

A pronoun and its referent must agree in number. Singular nouns require singular pronouns. Plural nouns require plural pronouns. Some examples follow.

The widow wanted her land back.

The farmers wanted their land back.

In the first sentence, the singular noun *widow* requires the singular pronoun *her*. In the second sentence, the plural noun *farmers* requires the plural pronoun *their*.

Most of the time pronoun agreement is often not a problem, but it can be when we try to find a pronoun to replace an indefinite pronoun.

An **indefinite pronoun** is a pronoun that refers to no one in particular. Here is a list of common indefinite pronouns that are always singular:

INDEFINITE PRONOUNS

one	nobody	each
anyone	anybody	either
everyone	everybody	neither
someone	somebody	

Study these sentences:

Incorrect: Each ~~of the boys~~ has their cap on backwards.

Correct: Each of the boys has his cap on backwards.

(***Each*** **requires a singular pronoun. Remember, cross out the prepositional phrase if you are confused about the subject.**)

Incorrect: Either Tammy or Tina will give me their ticket.

Correct: Either Tammy or Tina will give me her ticket.

(***Either*** **requires a singular pronoun.**)

In both speech and writing, to avoid being sexist we often use the plural *their* to refer to many indefinite pronouns that are singular. We say, for example, and it sounds perfectly right to our ear:

Someone left their coat on the desk.

Technically, this is wrong. *Their* is plural; *someone* is singular. On the other hand, *his*, the singular pronoun, is sexist:

Someone left his coat on the desk.

It is sexist because *someone* could be a female, a possibility the pronoun ignores.

The best way to correct an agreement problem is to rewrite. You can change to singular or plural. Both are correct. Here is an example:

Incorrect: Would everyone who ordered chicken raise their hands?

Correct: If you ordered chicken, raise your hand.

Correct: Would all the people who ordered chicken raise their hands?

Here is another example:

Incorrect: Did everyone in class get their seat assignments?

Correct: Did you get your seat assignment?

Correct: Did students get their seat assignments?

PRACTICING 3

Correct the agreement errors in the following sentences both ways that you've learned—by changing to the singular and changing to the plural.

1. Does everyone in the class have their notebooks?

Correct: _____

_____

Correct: _____

_____

2. If anyone needs a ride, they should let me know.

Correct: _____

_____

Correct: _____

_____

3. Is anybody taking their camera to the party?

Correct: _____

_____

Correct: _____

_____

4. Did somebody offer their seat to Mr. Kimble?

Correct: _____

_____

Correct: _____

_____

5. No one will be seated if they arrive after the show starts.

Correct: _____

_____

Correct: _____

_____

6. Would everyone please introduce themselves?

Correct: _____

_____

Correct: _____

_____

7. If someone has a good barbecue sauce recipe, they should
be required by law to share it.

Correct: _____

_____

Correct: _____

_____

8. Is anyone going to bring their partners to the reunion?

Correct: _____

_____

Correct: _____

_____

9. Everyone should hang their coats in the front closet.

Correct: _____

_____

Correct: _____

_____

10. Nobody should take themselves too seriously.

Correct: _____

_____

Correct: _____

_____

Sexist Use of Pronouns

You have just learned how to avoid sexism with indefinite pronouns. But sexism is even worse when a singular pronoun automatically assigns the male sex to professionals:

Every doctor should listen to his patients.

The use of *his* in the above sentence suggests that every doctor is a man, which is both sexist and untrue. On the other hand, using *his or her* is correct but clumsy. One solution is to make the whole sentence plural, using the neutral pronoun *their*. Here are the possible nonsexist choices:

Incorrect: Every doctor should listen to his patients.
Correct: Every doctor should listen to his or her patients.
Correct: Doctors should listen to their patients.

Their includes both men and women, and it is not as clumsy as *his or her*.
    If you are facing a pronoun agreement problem that you simply cannot rewrite in the plural, then use *his or her*. If the choice is between being sexist or being clumsy, it is better to be clumsy.

In a Nutshell

- Pronouns and their antecedents must agree in number.

- Avoid the sexist use of pronouns.

PRACTICING 4

Rewrite the following sentences to correct the pronoun agreement problem or the sexist bias.

1. No student on the social committee was willing to give up their vacation.

_____

_____

2. A newspaper reporter often uses his cellular phone.

_____

_____

3. People who have owned a Persian cat know that they are great pets.

_____

_____

4. As soon as a person realizes that they have been insulted, they leave.

_____

_____

5. A good neighbor mows their lawn regularly.

_____

_____

6. You may borrow either of those blouses if you promise to iron them.

_____

_____

7. One or the other of the girls must admit that they stole the cake.

_____

_____

8. Each of the nurses will buy their own ticket for the hospital's banquet.

_____

_____

9. Before someone learns to drive, they have to walk or take a bus.

_____

_____

10. Anyone who does not pay their health fee will not be given a flu shot.

_____

_____

Shifting Point of View

Writing is easier to read if it uses the same point of view throughout. You may choose a first person, second person, or third person point of view:

	First Person	**Second Person**	**Third Person**
SINGULAR	I	you	he, she, it, one
PLURAL	we	you	they

Here are some examples:

Incorrect: If a <u>person</u> finds a wallet with identification, <u>you</u> should return it to the owner.

Correct: When <u>you</u> find a wallet with identification, <u>you</u> should return it to the rightful owner.

or

When <u>one</u> finds a wallet with identification, <u>one</u> should return it to the rightful owner.

Here is another example containing many shifts:

> If <u>you're</u> unhappy, try taking a good hard look at <u>your</u> priorities. When <u>we</u> do that honestly, <u>we</u> can often see imbalances. <u>You</u> can be spending all <u>your</u> time working and not paying attention to the important people in your life. Is <u>one's</u> job really more important than <u>your</u> family? <u>We</u> say no, but then <u>we</u> accept the promotion that means working longer hours and on weekends. Think again about <u>your</u> priorities.

Here is the correction using *you*. *You*, *we*, or *one* would all be correct as long as the same point of view is used throughout with no shifts from one pronoun to another.

> If <u>you're</u> unhappy, try taking a good hard look at <u>your</u> priorities. When <u>you</u> do that honestly, <u>you</u> can often see imbalances. <u>You</u> can be spending all <u>your</u> time working and not paying attention to the important people in <u>your</u> life. Is <u>your</u> job really more important than <u>your</u> family? <u>You</u> say no, but then <u>you</u> accept the promotion that means working longer hours and on weekends. Think again about <u>your</u> priorities.

In a Nutshell

Avoid shifts in pronoun point of view. In other words, be consistent in your use of pronouns.

PRACTICING 5

Correct the pronoun shifts in the following sentences.

1. When I first visited the Louvre, you could see all the tourists heading toward the *Mona Lisa*.

2. Despite the fact that we are loyal and honest, you can't count on others being that way.

3. One should learn a little tact if they are a mother-in-law.

4. At our college, students have to study hard if you want top grades.

5. As you enter the building, the personnel office is on one's left.

6. If a person is going to graduate from college, they must practice good study habits.

7. You have to step back and take an objective look at yourself if a person wants to get over some bad habit.

8. If one is traveling to a strange state, you should buy a map.

9. If someone were to invent a cream that would dissolve body fat, you could become a millionaire.

10. We always look forward to the Fourth of July because you can cook out during the day and see fireworks at night.

UNIT TEST

Rewrite the following sentences to correct the pronoun errors.

1. Tanya told Mary she had to study hard.

   _____

   _____

2. They spread the rumor that Murray was suffering from flesh-eating bacteria.

   _____

   _____

3. Everyone who wants your picture in the yearbook should sign up today.

_____

_____

4. A surgeon should always reassure his patients.

_____

_____

5. In the counseling office they said I needed a cultural diversity course.

_____

_____

6. At the edge of the park it says, "Don't litter."

_____

_____

7. One of the people in line dropped their checkbook.

_____

_____

8. Each of my neighbors put their flags out on the Fourth of July.

_____

_____

9. Does anyone care about their car getting wet?

_____

_____

10. Either the leader or the others will pass me his ticket.

_____

_____

11. Bert paid for Ben and his dad to attend the game.

_____

_____

12. I love beautiful flowers that also have a fragrance, making you appreciate them.

_____

_____

13. All of us loved to hang out with Peter and Jim, but then he suddenly left town.

_____

_____

14. Although my father is an excellent preacher, my brother has no interest in it.

_____

_____

15. Neither of the boys care one hoot about sports.

_____

_____

16. Everybody thinks their country is the best.

_____

_____

UNIT TALKING ASSIGNMENT

A. Read the following sentences aloud to a classmate, who should catch the pronoun errors and tell you how to correct them. Try to reach agreement on all sentences.

1. Mary told Felice that her boss was too strict.
2. At the Career Center they suggested that Judy should be an architect.
3. Anybody who gets up will lose their seat.
4. If you have your health, one has everything.
5. Not only was the coat much too tight, it was also made of cheap material, which made Irene angry.
6. Merlin walked with a hot dog in one hand and a piece of carrot cake in the other, munching on it as he headed down the steps.
7. It clearly states that you must have your parents' signature.
8. As we walked into the movie, they told us that only the two front rows were unoccupied.

9. Nancy intended to tell her teacher that she had been rude.

10. Everyone wanted his ticket back.

B. Now reverse your roles. Again, try to reach agreement on all sentences.

1. Jane told Marguerite that her cousin would be at the meeting.

2. At the market they said the peaches were ripe.

3. Neither of the girls want to attend the wedding.

4. Every nurse should be kind to your patients.

5. As one enters the restaurant, it says, "No checks, please."

6. Neither of the grocery checkers ever smile.

7. They have a lot of freeway traffic in Los Angeles.

8. Each of the volunteers takes pride in their service to others.

9. Everyone scored at least 80 on their algebra test.

10. If we are aware of a problem, you should try to help.

UNIT WRITING ASSIGNMENT

Research shows that by age 18, a child has seen 18,000 people on television being strangled, stabbed, shot, drowned, run over, beaten to death, or otherwise killed. Do you think violence on television makes children more violent? Frame your argument in a discussible topic sentence. Back up your point with vivid details.

Pronoun Problems

"Him and I are good buddies."

nglish has three cases: subjective, objective, and possessive. Nouns do not change form when they are used as subjects or objects. They change form only in the possessive case:

Larry kissed Nancy.   (**Larry is the subject.**)

Nancy kissed Larry.   (**Larry is the object.**)

Larry's kisses were sweet.   (**The 's added to the noun Larry indicates that they are his kisses. He "possesses" them.**)

If we replace *Larry* with a pronoun, the pronoun is different in all three cases, the subjective, objective, and possessive:

He kissed Nancy.

Nancy kissed *him.*

His kisses were sweet.

If pronouns, like nouns, would only stay the same whether used as subjects or objects, English would be a far easier language to write and speak. Unfortunately, only the pronouns *it* and *you* take the same case and spelling whether they are used as subject or object.
Here are the pronouns in all three cases:

Subject pronouns	Object pronouns	Possessive pronouns	
I	me	my, mine	
you	you	your, yours	} SINGULAR
he	him	his	
she	her	hers	
we	us	our, ours	
you	you	your, yours	} PLURAL
they	them	theirs	

Case Problems

Because pronouns change case depending on how they are used, many of us often make case errors. Typically, we use a subject pronoun for an object pronoun, or the other way around. In the following sections we will discuss the correct use of subject pronouns, object pronouns, possessive pronouns, and reflexive pronouns.

Subject pronouns

Subject pronouns replace nouns used as subjects. Here are the rules for using subject pronouns.

Use a subject pronoun as the subject of a verb.

We usually use subject pronouns correctly, saying *I work at McDonald's*, not *Me work at McDonald's*. But we can run into problems with pronouns used in compound subjects.

Incorrect: Buddy and me made a pact.

Correct: Buddy and I made a pact.

Buddy and *I* form the compound subject of the verb *made*.

Incorrect: They and us can't get along.

Correct: They and we can't get along.

They and *we* form the compound subject of the verb *can't*.

To test whether you are using the correct pronoun in a compound subject, try each pronoun in the sentence separately. Your ear will tell you which is right. For example:

Buddy and (I, me) made a pact.

Test: I made a pact.
            Me made a pact.

Clearly, *Me made a pact* sounds wrong. The correct pronoun is therefore *I*. Try the test with another sentence:

They and (we, us) can't get along.

Test: We can't get along.
            Us can't get along.

Your ear tells you which pronoun is correct—*we*.

PRACTICING 1

Underline the correct pronoun in parentheses.

1. Legislation now protects (we, us) disabled students.

2. The picture was painted by three of us—Pete, Mabel, and (I, me).

3. For (we, us) nature lovers, the Sierras are like a church.

4. If it weren't for (he, him) and (I, me), you'd be in trouble.

5. Many of (we, us) math majors are afraid of English.

6. The volleyball team chose Terry and (her, she).

7. We stood right behind my dad and (them, they).

8. The wealthy aunt gave money to Laura and (he, him).

9. You can't stop us from voting for (they, them).

10. John and (me, I) often go hiking together.

Use a subject pronoun in comparisons.

In sentences using *than* or *as* to make a comparison, the second verb is usually omitted because we know what is meant. For example, in the sentence *Mary is more patient than I*, we really mean,

> Mary is more patient than I am patient.

To test whether you're using the right pronoun in a *than* or *as* sentence, simply complete the comparison. Here is another example:

> They are as tough as (us, we).

> **Test:**   They are as tough as us are tough.
> They are as tough as we are tough.

Your ear tells you that *we* is correct.

Use a subject pronoun after the verb to be.

If you rely on your ear to get the pronoun right after the verb *to be*, you will probably get it wrong. Here are some examples:

> **Incorrect:**   It is her speaking.
> **Correct:**   It is she speaking.

> **Incorrect:**   Was it them who swam to the island?
> **Correct:**   Was it they who swam to the island?

The correct sentences probably sound bizarre to your inner grammar ear. After all, most people say *it's me* rather than the grammatically correct *it's I*. In spoken language that usage is fine, but as we have often said in this book, Standard written English requires grammatical correctness.

If you think that the grammatically correct sentences don't sound right, you can always rewrite them to avoid the *it + to be + pronoun* construction. For instance:

> **Original:**   It is she speaking.
> **Rewrite:**   She is speaking.

Original: Was it they who swam to the island?

Rewrite: Did they swim to the island?

One good thing about talking or writing in English: You always have a choice.

In a Nutshell

- Use a subject pronoun as the subject of a verb.

- Use a subject pronoun in comparisons.

- Use a subject pronoun after the verb *to be*.

PRACTICING 2

In the blank provided, mark *C* if the italicized pronoun is correct and *NC* if it is not correct.

1. _____ Was that her making the decision?

2. _____ Yes, it was I who baked the cake.

3. _____ If I were them, I would pay the fine.

4. _____ It was supposed to be them who sat at the corner table.

5. _____ Would you like to be she?

6. _____ Who sent the E-mail? It was he.

7. _____ To be him would mean living in a fish bowl.

8. _____ If it had to be they, it had to be—that's fate for you.

9. _____ Yes, it was her who wrote the letter.

10. _____ Is that your mother over there? Yes, it is she.

Object pronouns

Object pronouns take the place of nouns used as objects. The object of a verb is the word that receives its action. For example, in the sentence

I kissed Mary.

the object of *kissed* is *Mary*, who received the kiss. If you used a pronoun in place of *Mary*, it would have to be in the objective case.

Correct: I kissed her.

Incorrect: I kissed she.

Although your ear is generally a good guide to the correct use of object pronouns, one trouble spot is the pronoun after a preposition.

Use an object pronoun after a preposition.

A pronoun that follows a preposition becomes its object and must be in the objective case.

Incorrect: I mentioned the problem to she and the landlady.

Correct: I mentioned the problem to her and the landlady.

If you do not know which pronoun to use in a sentence, simply try the pronoun by itself. Your ear will tell you if you've used the correct form. For example:

I mentioned the problem to (she, her) and the landlady.

Test: I mentioned the problem to she.

I mentioned the problem to her.

Your ear will tell you that *her* is correct.

The preposition that probably gives the most trouble with pronoun use is *between*. How many times in everyday speech have you heard these incorrect forms?

Incorrect	**Correct**
between you and I	between you and me
between John and he	between John and him
between Mary and she	between Mary and her
between you and he	between you and him
between they and the police	between them and the police
between he and she	between him and her

Because the incorrect form is so common in everyday speech, this is one usage where you simply cannot trust your ear. Just remember that *between* is a preposition, and an object pronoun must be used after a preposition. You must observe this ironclad rule of grammar in your writing and should learn to use it in speaking.

Ear Alert

In a Nutshell

- Use *me, you, him, us, it, her,* or *them* when the pronoun is an object.

- Use an object pronoun after a preposition.

PRACTICING 3

Underline the correct pronoun in parentheses.

1. They spoke of the secrets that existed between them and (he, him).

2. They gave the books to (him, he) and (me, I).

3. The minister spoke to the couple and (he, him) at great length.

4. Watch out! Stand behind Pete and (they, them).

5. That is a matter for (she, her) and (I, me) to discuss.

6. I told Mr. Faber that I had seen Jo's letter to the class and (me, I).

7. Without my uncle and (she, her) as guides, you'll get lost.

8. I live right next door to (her, she).

9. The person with (they, them) arrived from Iran yesterday.

10. Let's all vote for (she, her).

PRACTICING 4

Underline the correct pronoun in parentheses in the following sentences.

1. Between you and (I, me), the weather is turning ugly.

2. The great friendship between his dog and (him, he) lasted for ten years.

3. The secret must remain between (them, they) and our family.

4. If you don't want to cause serious trouble between (they, them) and (us, we), don't gossip.

5. Nothing will ever come between you and (I, me).

Possessive pronouns

Possessive pronouns are pronouns that show ownership or possession. A list of the possessive pronouns follows.

Possessive pronouns

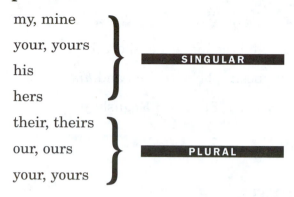

my, mine
your, yours
his
hers } **SINGULAR**

their, theirs
our, ours
your, yours } **PLURAL**

There are three common possessive pronoun errors:

- *It's/its*: The contraction *it's* (short for *it is*) is sometimes incorrectly used instead of *its* (meaning, belonging to *it*).

  Incorrect: The dog wagged it's tail.

  Correct: The dog wagged its tail.

  You can test the correctness of such a sentence by using the long, rather than the contracted, form of *it's* in a sentence.

  Test: The dog wagged it is tail.

  The mistake is now plainly visible.

- *Hers'*, *his'*, and *theirs'*: These words do not need an apostrophe. They are already possessive.

  Incorrect: That's hers'.

  Correct: That's hers.

  Incorrect: The tweed coat is his'.

  Correct: The tweed coat is his.

  Incorrect: The red sports car is theirs'.

  Correct: The red sports car is theirs.

- *Yourn/hisn*: These words are ungrammatical. They are not Standard English. The correct forms are *yours* and *his*.

  Incorrect: That cup of coffee is yourn.

  Correct: That cup of coffee is yours.

  Incorrect: That algebra book is hisn.

  Correct: That algebra book is his.

In a Nutshell

- *Its* is a possessive pronoun; *it's* is short for *it is*.

- Do not use an apostrophe with *hers* and *his*.

- *Yourn* and *hisn* is not Standard English.

PRACTICING 5

In the blank, write either *its* or *it's*, whichever is correct.

1. _____ disgusting to see teenagers smoking.

2. The ramshackle house, with _____ broken chimney, makes an excellent postcard.

3. I dialed the restaurant, but _____ line was busy.

4. What kind of music is it? _____ jazz.

5. _____ very selfish of her not to visit her grandmother in the hospital.

6. Why did you say, " _____ going to rain"?

7. From the day of _____ first clang, the bell became a symbol.

8. _____ smooth and powerful engine makes it an expensive car.

9. When _____ time to go, we'll let you know.

10. Don't worry; _____ only the first draft.

Reflexive pronouns

A **reflexive pronoun** refers back to the subject in the sentence. It clarifies meaning or adds emphasis.

I bought myself a pair of cowboy boots.	**(I bought the boots not for *him*, but for *myself*.)**
He made himself an omelet.	**(For no one else.)**
The architect himself checked the staircase.	**(The architect didn't send his assistant—he did it *himself*.)**

The reflexive pronouns are listed below:

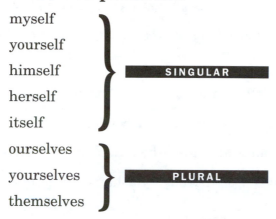

Reflexive pronouns

myself

yourself

himself   **SINGULAR**

herself

itself

ourselves

yourselves **PLURAL**

themselves

There are two common problems with reflexive pronouns. First, *hisself* is often used for *himself* and *theirself* for *themselves*. These are non-standard words like *ain't* and don't exist except in slang.

Incorrect:	He drives hisself to work.
Correct:	He drives himself to work.

Incorrect:	They surprised theirself.
Correct:	They surprised themselves.

The second common problem with reflexive pronouns is the use of *me* (an objective pronoun) instead of *myself* (the reflexive pronoun).

Incorrect:	I bought me a new pair of boots.
Correct:	I bought myself a new pair of boots.

In a Nutshell

- *Hisself* and *theirself* are not standard words.

- Do not use *me* in place of *myself*.

PRACTICING 6

Underline the correct reflexive pronoun in parentheses for each sentence below.

1. They blamed (theirselves, themselves) for the dismal outcome.

2. They congratulated (theirself, themselves) on a job well done.

3. He spoke at the ceremony (himself, hisself).

4. Benny spilled grape juice on (himself, hisself).

5. They (theirselves, themselves) speak highly of the coach.

6. They bought (theirselves, themselves) steak dinners to celebrate.

7. John pulled (himself, hisself) out of the pool.

8. I bought (me, myself) a new car.

9. Why can't they carve the pumpkin (theirselves, themselves)?

10. He should be thoroughly ashamed of (himself, hisself).

Pesky Pronouns

Some pronouns are pesky—they give everyone trouble. Among the peskiest pronouns are *who/whom*, *who's/whose*, *who/which/that*, *this/that*, and *these/those*.

Who/whom

Two of the peskiest pronouns are *who* and *whom*.

Use who as a subject pronoun.
Who may be used in place of the following pronouns:

Subject Pronouns

REPLACE WITH WHO

I

you

he

she

we

they

Who is in class? (*She* is in class.)

Who is going to speak? (*He* is going to speak.)

Use whom as you would an object pronoun.

Object Pronouns

REPLACE WITH WHOM

me   us

you   them

him

her

Whom do you love? (I love *him*.)

To whom do I owe an apology? (I owe an apology to *him*.)

If you don't know whether to use *who* or *whom* in a question, try answering the question using *he*, *she*, *him*, *her*, or *them*. For example:

(Who, whom) do you know?

Test: I know him.
      I know he.

Whom is therefore correct.
    To apply the test to a statement, you have to turn the sentence around:

I know the detective to (who, whom) he confessed.

Test: He confessed to she.
      He confessed to her.

Whom is the correct choice.

In a Nutshell

Who is always used as a subject; *whom* is always used as an object.

PRACTICING 7

Fill in the blanks below with either *who* or *whom*.

1. _____ are you referring to?

2. I spoke to a loan officer _____ was very

   helpful.

3. Many of the writers _____ my teacher adores are

   dead.

4. The game of life is best played by the person _____

   has the best sense of humor.

5. They knew no one _____ matched that

   description.

6. As to _____ she meant, we could not say for the life

of us.

7. Know _____ you are dealing with.

8. I saw a man _____ danced with his wife in Chicago.

9. Ask not for _____ the bell tolls.

10. He says he knows many people _____ are very

stubborn.

Who's/whose

Who's is short for *who is; whose* shows possession. Here are some examples:

Incorrect:	They wondered who's car this was.
Correct:	They wondered whose car this was.

Incorrect:	I know whose to blame.
Correct:	I know who's to blame.

To test *who's/whose*, simply write out *who's* as *who is*:

They wondered who's car this was.

Test: They wondered who is car this was.
They wondered whose car this was.

Whose is obviously correct.

In a Nutshell

Whose shows possession; *who's* is short for *who is*.

PRACTICING 8

Fill in the blanks with either *who's* or *whose*.

1. _____ ball is this?

2. He's the man at _____ house we had dinner and

_____ responsible for the neighborhood's block party.

3. You may well wonder _____ life this is and

_____ destiny is at stake here.

4. _____ at the door?

5. He asked for the name of the person _____ the boss.

6. _____ paying for the birthday cake?

7. _____ locker is this?

8. The student in _____ wallet the money was found never appeared.

9. Our neighbor, in _____ garage the lawn mower was kept, moved away.

10. I haven't a clue _____ tennis shoes these are.

Who, which, and that

Knowing when to use *who*, *which*, and *that* is easy if you remember the following rules:

- Use *who* to refer to people and animals and *which* to refer to things.

  Lot's wife was the woman who looked back. (not <u>which</u>)

  Burt, who is a black lab, loves the water. (not <u>which</u>)

  Please return my book, which I left on the table.

  Please get the towels, which are still in the dryer.

  The Smiths, who live next door to us, are really helpful.

- *That* can refer either to a person or a thing.

  Use the tools that can do the job.

  The jury that convicted him was fair.

In a Nutshell

- Use *who* to refer to people and animals.
- Use *which* to refer to things.
- *That* can refer to either a person or a thing.

PRACTICING 9

Fill in the blanks below with the appropriate relative pronoun (*who*, *which*, or *that*).

1. The man _____ spoke at the meeting was quite convincing.

2. _____ among you will cast the first stone?

3. Jumping to conclusions _____ are wrong won't help this case.

4. The people _____ helped the most spoke the least.

5. I am monarch of all _____ I survey.

6. The chairs, _____ both have broken legs, are in the kitchen.

7. My cat, Millie, _____ is 14, is starting to show her age.

8. My dog, _____ is 9, still acts like a puppy.

9. Treman Park, _____ is part of the state park system, has several waterfalls.

This/that and these/those

The pronouns *this/that* (singular) and *these/those* (plural) are used to point to or single out something.

I just love *this* book.	**(A particular book is singled out.)**
Don't you dare eat *those* cookies.	**(Particular cookies are singled out.)**

This and *these* refer to something nearby, whereas *that* and *those* refer to something farther away.

I love petting *this* cat.

but

Would you mind walking across the room to bring me *that* blanket?

Two kinds of problems can occur in the use of *this/that* and *these/those*. First, an object pronoun is used instead of *this*, *these*, or *those*.

Incorrect:	*Them* doughnuts are fattening.	(***Them* is an object pronoun.)**
Correct:	*Those* doughnuts are fattening.	

Or, sometimes, the word *here* or *there* is added by mistake.

Incorrect:	*This here* yard is full of weeds.	(***Here* is unnecessary.)**
Correct:	*This* yard is full of weeds.	

Incorrect:	*That there* house needs painting.	(*There* is unnecessary.)	
Correct:	*That* house needs painting.		

In a Nutshell

- Never use *here* or *there* after a demonstrative pronoun (as in *this here book*.)

- Never use *them* in place of *these* or *those*.

PRACTICING 10

Underline the correct pronoun in parentheses.

1. (Those, them) ducks are quacking nonstop.

2. Please take (this/that) package to Mrs. Jones.

3. (This here, this) suitcase is too heavy to carry.

4. Did Peter borrow (them, those) roller skates?

5. There is nothing wrong with Marcos carrying the painting across the street to (this, that) house.

6. Why don't you sit down and play (this here, this) piano?

7. Take (this, that) one right next to me.

8. If (that, this) present weather continues, you'd better buy a raincoat.

9. Be polite to (these, those) women standing over there.

10. (That, that there) rug was woven in India.

UNIT TEST

In the blank provided, mark *C* if the sentence is correct and *NC* if there is a pronoun error.

1. _____ Narbeh and me decided to climb Mt. Whitney.

2. _____ For whom did she work last year?

3. _____ Who did you kiss at the prom?

4. _____ A long time ago, we mentioned the letter to Mom and she.

5. _____ As far she and me are concerned, forget it.

6. _____ Between Bob and him, the choice is easy.

7. _____ I wonder to whom she told that story.

8. _____ Was it your idea to exchange them socks?

9. _____ Them carrots taste too salty.

10. _____ Why did you let him paint the door all by hisself?

11. _____ Just between you and me, the Dodgers will lose.

12. _____ I bought me some new shoes.

13. _____ Chris and me have joined a car pool.

14. _____ They are every bit as disgusted as we.

15. _____ I want that lovely vase, but it's side is cracked.

UNIT TALKING ASSIGNMENT

Get together with a classmate. One of you should read aloud Part A of the selection that follows, sentence by sentence, stressing each underlined pronoun error while the other corrects it. Stop after each sentence to decide whether it is correct or how it should be corrected.

Part A

One of my favorite activities is biking because I learn from nature, and also its good exercise. Bikers say that a person can learn a lot when they visit new places on a bicycle. When my friend Fred and me first biked through Colorado, I felt as if I had entered a whole new world. The mountains and canyons seemed to tell a very ancient story. For instance, Snow Bird Peak, rising majestically out of the earth, seemed to say that human beings like Fred and I are insignificant compared to the power of nature.

Part B

At the same time that we were seeing so much beauty, we were also exercising my leg, arm, and stomach muscles. The aerobic part of the exercise was helpful as well. Its quite challenging to pedal up a steep grade. I can't think of another sport that would have allowed Fred and I to experience so much beauty and such good exercise while costing so little money. All college students should take a biking trip and find out for theirself what a great experience and what good exercise it is.

UNIT WRITING ASSIGNMENT

Write a paragraph describing the most unpleasant trip you ever took and what you learned from it. Pay special attention to pronoun use.

Distinguishing Between Adjectives and Adverbs

> **"**Gertie dances real good.**"**

Using your ear for grammar to help you write is, for the most part, a good strategy. When it comes to the correct use of adjectives and adverbs, however, your ear is likely to be too infected with street-talk to be trusted.

Indeed, adjectives and adverbs are often misused in casual speech. The following are some typical sentences you might overhear in public:

Gertie dances real good.

The Olympic contestants swam terrific.

The guards told us to walk slow.

That remark bothered me considerable.

All of us were real tired.

If these sentences sound right to you, your ear is leading you astray. Here are the sentences correctly written:

Ear Alert

Gertie dances really well.

The Olympic contestants swam terrifically.

The guards told us to walk slowly.

That remark bothered me considerably.

All of us were really tired.

No matter what your ear tells you, these sentences are grammatically correct. This unit will help you to use adjectives and adverbs correctly in your writing.

Adjectives and Adverbs

Adjectives and adverbs are **modifiers**, words that describe and explain. **Adjectives** describe a noun or a pronoun by narrowing it down to a specific one, such as in the following cases:

I adore that purple hat.	**(Which hat? The *purple* one.)**
She certainly seems happy.	**(What kind of person does she seem? A *happy* one.)**
The milk smells sour.	**(How does the milk smell? It smells *sour*)**

Adverbs describe verbs, adjectives, and other adverbs in the following ways:

- how

- when

- where

- to what extent

Here are some examples:

She spoke very excitedly.	(***Very*** **tells how she spoke—describes the adverb *excitedly*.**)
I'm going now.	(***Now*** **tells when I'm going—describes the verb *going*.**)
I put the book there.	(***There*** **tells where the book was put—describes the verb *put*.**)
Orson Welles became excessively fat.	(***Excessively*** **tells to what extent Welles became fat—describes the adjective *fat*.**)

Many—but not all—adverbs end in *-ly*. Indeed, many adjectives can be turned into adverbs simply by adding *-ly*. Some typical examples follow.

Adjective	Adverb
careful	carefully
real	really
most	mostly
forceful	forcefully

However, some of the most commonly used adverbs do not end in -*ly*. Here are some examples:

Walk *fast*.

He is *very* patient.

She is *too* thin.

They are *always* late.

She is leaving *tomorrow*.

In a Nutshell

- Adjectives describe nouns and pronouns.

- Adverbs describe verbs, adjectives, and other adverbs.

- Many—but not all—adverbs end in -*ly*.

PRACTICING 1

Complete the sentences below with an appropriate modifier—either an adjective or an adverb—from the following list. Each word should be used only once.

sadly	immediately
soon	slowly
silently	dreadful
terribly	hot
playful	most

In the parentheses at the end of each sentence, identify the modifier as an adjective or adverb.

1. The telephone company hired Bob _____.

   (_____)

2. My bath water was _____. (_____)

3. It was a _____ call. (_____)

4. Thereafter he sat _____. (_____)

5. The next mile of the road was _____ rough. (_____)

6. We drew abreast the other motorcycle _____. (_____)

7. The waitress looked _____ at the rain. (_____)

8. The _____ puppies romped in the grass. (_____)

9. She _____ picked up her suitcase and walked away. (_____)

10. Tom complained _____ often. (_____)

PRACTICING 2

Underline the correct modifier in parentheses—adjective or adverb—in each sentence below.

1. The old man crossed the railroad tracks (slow, slowly).

2. His fingernails looked (awful, awfully) dirty.

3. He (nimble, nimbly) climbed down the mine shaft.

4. The birds flew away, chirping (angry, angrily).

5. He (near, nearly) struck a boulder.

6. He had a bad cold and was feeling (miserable, miserably).

7. John examined the roof (careful, carefully).

8. My friend felt (complete, completely) alone in his poverty.

9. The teacher prepared a (clever, cleverly) list of words for the spelling test.

10. The engine hummed (smooth, smoothly).

PRACTICING 3

Change the italicized adjective to an adverb; you will need to rewrite the sentence.

Example: Have you noticed her *elegant* walk?

Answer: Have you noticed how *elegantly* she walks?

1. Mark is *happy* to speak.

_____

2. Dogs can be *noisy* barkers.

_____

3. His performance was *admirable*.

_____

4. What a *tight* jacket!

_____

5. He's a *slow* walker.

_____

6. He wrote a *poor* essay.

_____

7. The man was a *glib* talker.

_____

8. Her arrival was *unexpected*.

_____

9. He gave her an *intimate* hug.

_____

10. It was a *quiet* moan.

_____

Past participles used as adjectives

The past participles of verbs may also be used as adjectives. Consider the verb *mash*:

Please mash the potatoes.   (*mash* = present)

I mashed the potatoes yesterday.   (***mashed*** = past)

I have mashed the potatoes every day.   (***have mashed*** = past participle)

These mashed potatoes are good.   (***mashed*** = adjective)

Here are other examples of past participles used as adjectives:

broken bones

aged dog

rented car

frozen food

torn jacket

Ear Alert

A common problem with using past participles as adjectives is dropping the *-d/-ed* or *-n/-en* ending. We do this so often, especially in rapid speech, that the mistake usually goes unnoticed. A dropped ending in writing, however, is always obvious. Look at these examples:

Dropped ending: We ate mash potatoes with butter.
Correct: We ate mashed potatoes with butter.

Dropped ending: I was sad to see those broke toys.
Correct: I was sad to see those broken toys.

In a Nutshell

Don't let your ear trick you into dropping the *-d/-ed* or *n/-en* ending when you write a past participle.

PRACTICING 4

Correct the misused past participles in the sentences below.

1. He wept about his dash hopes. _____

2. Watch out for the broke glass! _____

3. His pants were tore. _____

4. The potatoes are all peel. _____

5. The eraser of the pencil looked chew. _____

6. He had not practice enough. _____

7. That's not an excuse absence. _____

8. I looked through the broke window. _____

9. He said the fish was fresh-froze. _____

10. I'll have two hard-boil eggs, please. _____

11. Dad wore a borrow tie. _____

12. They quarreled over some spoke words. _____

Comparisons

Adjectives and adverbs are often used to make comparisons between two things. The rules for making comparisons are straightforward:

■ For an adjective or adverb of one syllable, add *-er*.

My uncle Bob is *rich.*

Uncle John is *richer.*   **(one-syllable adjective)**

He spoke *fast.*

She spoke *faster.*   **(one-syllable adverb)**

■ For an adjective or adverb of more than one syllable that does not end in *y,* add *more.*

This is an *affordable* car.

This is a *more affordable* car.   **(adjective of more than one syllable)**

The man snored *loudly.*

His wife, however, snored *more loudly.*   **(adverb of more than one syllable)**

■ For an adjective or adverb that ends in *y,* drop the *y* and add *-ier* in the comparative.

The road to the farm was *icy.*

The road to the mountains was *icier.*

Jerry is *funny.*

Mary is *funnier.*

PRACTICING 5

Write the comparative form of each word listed below.

Example: feverish   *more feverish*

          fresh   *fresher*

1. ugly   _____

2. hateful   _____

3. junky   _____

4. marvelous   _____

5. hot   _____

6. silly   _____

7. silent   _____

8. lucky   _____

9. spicy   _____

10. thorough   _____

Double comparisons

A common mistake often heard in everyday speech is the **double comparison**, using both *-er* and *more*.

Incorrect: Janet's writing is more neater than Mary's.
Correct: Janet's writing is neater than Mary's.

Incorrect: I spoke more louder than you.
Correct: I spoke louder than you.

PRACTICING 6

Rewrite the following sentences to correct the comparisons.

1. You carry the more heavier suitcase.

   _____

2. If I study hard, I should do more better in math.

   _____

3. He was a more crueler king than his predecessor.

   _____

4. Who was the more nicer of the two?

_____

5. The wind was terrifyinger than the rain.

_____

6. The cheese is more fresher than the salami.

_____

7. My brother was more badlier hurt than my sister.

_____

8. When can you give me a more better answer?

_____

9. Working at three jobs was difficulter than I
thought.

_____

10. The cut was more deeper than the doctor
expected.

_____

Using Superlatives

The comparative form of adjectives and adverbs is used to express a difference between two things.

The brown suitcase is strong.

The black suitcase is stronger.   **(comparative)**

To express differences among three or more things, you must use the superlative form of an adjective or adverb.

The brown suitcase is strong.

The black suitcase is stronger.   **(comparative)**

The blue suitcase is strongest.   **(superlative)**

Mother speaks fast.

Father speaks faster.   **(comparative)**

Brother speaks fastest of all.   **(superlative)**

The simple rules for changing adjectives and adverbs into the superlative form follow.

■ For an adverb or adjective of one syllable, add *-est*.

wild → wilder → wildest

glad → gladder → gladdest   **(Note that the "d" is doubled.)**

tall → taller → tallest

She was saddest of all the relatives there.

■ For an adverb or adjective that ends in *y*, drop the *y* and add *-iest*.

silly → sillier → silliest

tiny → tinier → tiniest

pretty → prettier → prettiest

He was the luckiest of them all.

■ For an adjective or adverb of two or more syllables that does not end in *y*, add the word *most*.

dreadful → more dreadful → most dreadful

cheerful → more cheerful → most cheerful

interesting → more interesting → most interesting

She is the most cheerful person in the morning.

PRACTICING 7

In the blanks provided, write the correct superlative forms of the words below.

1. ugly _____

2. disappointed _____

3. meek _____

4. rich _____

5. pushy _____

6. snappy _____

7. regretful _____

8. ripe _____

9. short _____

10. slick _____

Problems with superlatives

When you use superlatives, watch out for these two common errors of everyday speech:

- Use the superlative only when you are speaking of *more than two* things.

  Incorrect: She is the most beautiful of the two sisters.

  Correct: She is the more beautiful of the two sisters.

  Incorrect: This is the riskiest of the two choices.

  Correct: This is the riskiest of the three choices.

  or

  This is the riskier of the two choices.

- Do not use both an *-est* or an *-iest* ending and *most*.

  Incorrect: She is the most unkindest person.

  Correct: She is the unkindest person.

  Incorrect: He is the most trendiest dresser.

  Correct: He is the trendiest dresser.

In a Nutshell

- Use a comparative adjective or adverb to compare two things.

- Form most comparatives by adding *-er*, *-ier*, or *more*.

- Use a superlative adjective or adverb to compare three or more things.

- Form most superlatives by adding *-est*, *-iest*, or *most*.

PRACTICING 8

Rewrite the following sentences to correct the errors in forming the superlative.

1. The is the most beautifulest rose I have ever seen.

_____

_____

2. That movie is the fascinatingest one I've seen this
    year.

_____

_____

3. Give the piece of pie to the most biggest football player.

_____

_____

4. My mother was one of the most wisest women imaginable.

_____

_____

5. Just because she is the most oldest, my sister gets more
    spending money.

_____

_____

6. Have you chosen the most fastest runner yet?

_____

_____

7. Maggie is definitely the interestingest of the three
    girls.

_____

_____

8. Jake is the most stingiest roommate he ever had.

_____

_____

9. How can you say that our legislators are the corruptest
    people in the state?

_____

_____

10. Go down Maxwell Street, and you'll find the most poorest
     people you have ever seen.

_____

_____

PRACTICING 9

For the following sentences, first decide if a comparative or superlative form is needed. Then write the correct form.

Example: All of us wanted to climb the (tall) <u>taller</u> of the two towers.

1. It was the (frightening) _____ story I have ever heard.

2. Of the two deans, Smith was the (reasonable) _____.

3. My high school graduation was the (long) _____ day of my life.

4. Ann's wedding was (expensive) _____ than Mary's.

5. The desert is much (dry) _____ than the beach.

6. Of the two wrestlers, Moe was the (fat) _____.

7. Aunt Ethel was the (secretive) _____ relative in our family.

8. Think about your three options, then decide on the (good) _____.

9. What was the (nice) _____ experience you had in elementary school?

10. Sardines are (oily) _____ than salmon.

Using Good/Well and Bad/Badly

Most adjectives and adverbs follow the basic rules for forming comparatives and superlatives that we have just described. A few, however, have irregular forms. The most troublesome are *good/well* and *bad/badly*.

	Comparative	**Superlative**
good	better	best
well	better	best
bad	worse	worst
badly	worse	worst

Good is an adjective; *well* is an adverb (unless you are talking about someone's health). Here are examples.

Correct:	This is a good bicycle.	(***Good*** **is an adjective describing** ***bicycle.***)
Incorrect:	She rides good.	
Correct:	She rides well.	(***Well*** **is an adverb telling how she** ***rides.***)
Incorrect:	I don't feel good.	
Correct:	I don't feel well.	(**Use** ***well*** **to describe someone's health.**)

Bad is an adjective; *badly* is an adverb. A common mistake made in everyday speech is to use *badly* to describe emotions when *bad* should be used.

Incorrect:	I feel badly that we were late.
Correct:	I feel bad that we were late.

To say *I feel badly* is to mean that your sense of touch is bad—perhaps your fingers are numb.

There is no such word as *bestest* or *worsest*. The correct form is either *best* or *worst*.

In a Nutshell

- *Good* is an adjective; *well* is used as an adverb unless you're talking about someone's health.

- *Bad* is an adjective; *badly* is an adverb.

- To say *I feel badly* means something is wrong with your sense of touch.

PRACTICING 10

Write either *good* or *well* in the blanks provided.

1. All the sophomores on the team swam _____.

2. Even the honor students did not do _____ on the final test.

3. His coat was made of _____ leather.

4. It was obvious that she was not feeling _____.

5. This cream is _____ for your complexion.

6. I have been _____ to you lately.

7. You must try to do _____ on your final exam.

8. He meant _____ when he gave us that _____ advice.

9. You know very _____ when I mean!

10. You will do _____ if you try your best.

PRACTICING 11

In the blanks below, insert either *bad* or *badly*.

1. He spoke very _____ for an English major.

2. She felt _____ for her father.

3. I felt _____ that we lost the game.

4. His manners are very _____.

5. The crew sailed the first leg of the race _____.

6. I'm _____ sick with the flu.

7. The flu shot made me feel _____.

8. They hoisted the flag very _____ .

9. No matter how _____ they feel, they are still right.

10. I'm _____ in need of a good friend.

UNIT TEST

Correct the following sentences.

1. Mary's essay is the bestest in the class.

_____

_____

2. She scribbled her signature quick.

_____

_____

3. The beggar looked envious at the mountain of food.

_____

_____

4. John was the most patient of the two men.

_____

_____

5. He lied unashamed.

_____

_____

6. Billy folded his blanket most carefulliest.

_____

_____

7. It is best for you to walk home rather than ride.

_____

_____

8. Feeling gratefully that she had escaped, Fran wept.

_____

_____

9. The speech was the baddest he had ever given.

_____

_____

10. Mark said he had been cured and was now feeling good.

_____

_____

UNIT TALKING ASSIGNMENT

In the following series of sentences about leasing versus buying, work with a partner to fill in the blanks with an appropriate adverb or adjective selected from the list below. You may use each word more than once.

heavy	very good	wholeheartedly
unquestionably	smarter	definitely
little	good	economically
cheaper	quickly	lately
better	common	confident
constantly		

1. Because mechanical things get outdated so _____,

leasing items is becoming _____ than buying them.

2. In a number of states, it is actually _____ to lease a
   car than to own one.

3. Leasing a car feels _____ because the lessee does not
   have to worry _____ about trade-in values or maintenance costs.

4. Leasing is advertised to appeal to those who want to live
   _____ without being burdened by every little detail of
   keeping up a car.

5. The leasing trend is _____ invading many other
   _____ manufactured goods besides cars.

6. For instance, maintenance and service problems for
   such _____ appliances as freezers, stoves,
   dishwashers, washers, dryers, and air-conditioners have
   _____ promoted "temporary use" rather than
   "permanent ownership."

7. I have to agree that leasing a car is _____ than
   buying one.

8. Next year my lease will be up, and I shall then _____
   lease a brand new car of my choice.

9. I feel _____ about never having to drive
   an old car.

10. I _____ agree with those who believe that leasing
    helps one get rid of the _____ curse of possessions.

UNIT WRITING ASSIGNMENT

Beginning with one of the topic sentences listed below, develop a
paragraph that is vivid and clear. Pay special attention to your use of
adverbs and adjectives.

1. Our love for machines lessens our love for human
   beings.
2. Preserving the wilderness is our hope for planet Earth.
3. People who don't have pets are missing a lot.
4. I have found that failures teach me more than successes.
5. I have learned that it is not wise to burn your bridges.

Dangling and Misplaced Modifiers

> **"**After watching the movie, the sky turned black and began to rain.**"**

A modifier is a word or phrase that describes—you learned that in Unit 10. Modifiers are either adjectives or adverbs, or words or phrases that function as adjectives or adverbs. What a modifier describes in a sentence depends not only on what it says, but also on where it is located.

Panting, the bus pulled away just as Mary arrived.

Here *panting* is a modifier, but because of its place in the sentence, it modifies *bus* rather than *Mary*. Such a modifier is said to *dangle*.

Dangling Modifiers

A **dangling modifier** is one whose place in a sentence causes it to modify the wrong word. For instance, if a modifier begins a sentence, the word it modifies must come immediately after it. Otherwise, the modifier will be unconnected to the word the writer meant it to modify. In short, it will dangle. Here are some examples:

Dangling: Walking home that day, the sun seemed unusually warm.

Dangling: Breathless, the plane pulled away just as Frank reached the gate.

Dangling: Having reached the age of six, my grandfather marched me off to grade school.

Dangling: Aggressive, the job suited Paul perfectly.

To correct these sentences, simply place the word being modified immediately after the modifier.

Correct: Walking home that day, I thought the sun seemed unusually warm.

or

As I walked home that day, the sun seemed unusually warm.

Correct: Breathless, Frank reached the gate just as the plane pulled away.

Correct: Having reached the age of six, I was marched off to grade school by my grandfather.

or

I was marched off to grade school by my grandfather when I reached the age of six.

Correct: Aggressive, Paul suited the job perfectly.

In a Nutshell

Correct dangling modifiers by rearranging or adding words so that the modifier clearly refers to the right word.

PRACTICING 1

Rewrite these sentences, each of which contains a dangling modifier.

1. Fat and ugly, I decided not to buy the bulldog.

_____

_____

2. Lying in the drawer, Denise finally found her gold watch.

_____

_____

3. Worn out from hiking, the alarm clock didn't wake me up.

_____

_____

4. Being newly painted, I did not mind paying $4,000 for the car.

_____

_____

5. As a mother of twins, my washing machine is always running.

_____

_____

6. After taking our seats, the Ice Capades started off with a waltz.

_____

_____

7. Jumping through fiery hoops, the audience went wild over the circus dogs.

_____

_____

8. When shredded and salted, you will enjoy the taste of Russian cabbage.

_____

_____

9. Shining brightly, I gazed at the stars.

_____

_____

10. Flying to New York, the Empire State Building gleamed below.

_____

_____

Misplaced Modifiers

A modifier tends to modify the nearest noun. For example, notice how the meaning of the following sentence changes as we move the modifier *only*.

She went into the pool wearing her only bikini.	**(She owned only one *bikini*. Only is modifying *bikini*.)**
She went into the pool wearing only her bikini.	**(She wore nothing else but a bikini. *Only* is modifying *wearing*.)**

If a modifier is too far from the word it is meant to modify, it may give the sentence an unintended, funny meaning. Here are some examples of misplaced modifiers:

Misplaced: We could watch the stars sitting on the balcony.

Misplaced: My grandmother showed us how to sew a quilt with an encouraging smile.

Misplaced: I stood in the cold stream and caught a fish without waders.

Because of a misplaced modifier, we have *stars sitting on the balcony, quilts with an encouraging smile*, and *a fish without waders*. A misplaced modifier is corrected by rewriting the sentence. You must reword the modifier or move it closer to the word it modifies. Here are possible corrections:

Sitting on the balcony, we could watch the stars.

With an encouraging smile, my grandmother showed us how to sew a quilt.

I stood without waders in the cold stream and caught a fish.

or

Without waders, I stood in the cold stream and caught a fish.

To avoid the confusion of misplaced modifiers, always place a modifier immediately before the word it is meant to modify. This is especially true of one-word modifiers such as *almost, even, hardly, nearly, only*, and *often*. Because these words limit what follows, where they occur in a sentence is important. Remember the bikini example at the beginning of this section. Here is another example:

He just washed the dishes.   **(He did it a moment ago.)**

He washed just the dishes.   **(He didn't do the pots.)**

In a Nutshell

Avoid misplaced modifiers by placing modifiers as close as possible to the words they describe.

PRACTICING 2

First, underline the misplaced modifier in each sentence below. Then rewrite the sentence so that the modifier is correctly placed.

Example: I borrowed a ballpoint pen to write a letter <u>that didn't work.</u>

Answer: <u>To write a letter, I borrowed a ballpoint pen that didn't work.</u>

1. Mimi fed her dog on the porch she had received for Christmas.

_____

_____

2. A pilot since World War II in 1995, he received an award
   for long service.

   _____

   _____

3. The waiters served French pastries to customers on
   expensive bone china.

   _____

   _____

4. Caroline could not attend the dance in her lovely new
   off-the-shoulder gown with a broken foot.

   _____

   _____

5. Francine nearly did 20 sit-ups for one-half hour every
   morning.

   _____

   _____

6. John Henry School needs volunteers to read to their
   students badly.

   _____

   _____

7. Peter is canvassing the neighborhood for voters dressed in
   an Uncle Sam costume.

   _____

   _____

8. We saw many deer driving to the country.

   _____

   _____

9. We drank ten gallons of cranberry juice with relish.

   _____

   _____

10. At 10:00 A.M. the students heard that an earthquake had
    hit on television.

    _____

    _____

PRACTICING 3

Underline the dangling and misplaced modifiers in the following paragraph. Then rewrite those sentences correctly in the spaces below. You should find four errors.

An Afternoon by the Lake

It was July, and we were out of school. Having finished our chores and changed into our bathing suits, the lake seemed to invite us to come down and feel its coolness. My mind was only fixed on two things—swimming and what fun we would have. We ran to the lake and plunged into the cool water. We stayed until past dinner. But after explaining how much fun we had, my mother didn't punish me. To this day, I connect beautiful vacations with a lake in my mind.

1. _____

   _____

2. _____

   _____

3. _____

   _____

4. _____

   _____

UNIT TEST

The following sentences contain either a dangling or a misplaced modifier. Correct the sentences by rewriting them.

1. Having already waited an hour for the traffic to die down, our car wouldn't start.

   _____

   _____

2. After sticking my card key into the slot, the gate opened automatically.

   _____

   _____

3. Purring, the table was upset by the cat.

_____

_____

4. A lovely rainbow arched across the sky, driving after the rain.

_____

_____

5. We finally found her ring during our lunch break in the desk.

_____

_____

6. Rolling on wheels, I steered the suitcase down the hill.

_____

_____

7. Thinking about this poem, the meaning never was clear to me.

_____

_____

8. Drifting to sleep, my plaid sheets felt clean and cool.

_____

_____

9. Mr. Smith took the broken pipes to the dump in his truck.

_____

_____

10. Do not eat the brownie until completely baked.

_____

_____

UNIT TALKING ASSIGNMENT

Pair up with a partner. Each of you should alternate reading a sentence while the other corrects it, if necessary, in the space below. Decide what kind of error you have found. You should find four dangling or misplaced modifiers.

Children should live free from fear. Fear in a child's life has no redeeming qualities; it does not make a child stronger, nor does it teach the child how to be more independent. One of a child's worst fears comes from watching parents fight. Arriving home from work, little Freddy is afraid that Dad will start a fight with Mom.

So Freddy whispers a silent prayer that his parents will be peaceful under his breath. Children not only fear quarrels between their parents, they also fear snakes and spiders. For instance, if a child is in bed, ready for sleep, but sees a black spider crawling out of the corner of her eye, she may panic and have terrible nightmares the rest of the night. Again, fear of this kind is not good for the child's development. Perhaps a child's worst fear is the fear of abandonment. To feel safe, secure, and protected by their parents is crucial. Some children only feel secure when they finally grow up and have children of their own. When bringing up children, fear must be removed by parents.

1. _____

_____

2. _____

_____

3. _____

_____

4. _____

_____

UNIT WRITING ASSIGNMENT

Write a paragraph agreeing or disagreeing with the idea that "College is not for everyone." Begin with a discussible topic sentence and support it with appropriate facts and examples. Check your writing for misplaced or dangling modifiers.

UNIT 12
Using Prepositions

> **"**The plane flew above the cloud, behind the cloud, around the cloud, below the cloud, beneath the cloud, beside the cloud, beyond the cloud, into the cloud, near the cloud, outside the cloud, over the cloud, past the cloud, through the cloud, toward the cloud, under the cloud, and finally dived underneath the cloud.**"**

A **preposition** is a word that shows the relationship between two things. In the example above, the prepositions show the relationships between a plane and a cloud. Indeed, one informal definition of the preposition is anything an airplane can do to a cloud. This, however, is not a complete definition, as our list of common prepositions makes clear:

about	beside	inside	to
above	besides	like	toward
across	between	near	under
after	beyond	of	underneath
against	by	off	until
along	despite	on	up
among	down	out	with
around	during	outside	within
at	except	over	without
before	for	past	
behind	from	since	
below	in	through	
beneath	into	throughout	

Some prepositions consist of more than one word. Here is a list of the most common multiword prepositions:

along with	in place of
because of	in spite of
due to	instead of
except for	on account of
in addition to	out of
in case of	up to
in front of	with the exception of

179

PRACTICING 1

Without consulting the lists on page 179, place a check mark next to each preposition. Leave the other kinds of words unchecked.

1. _____ behind

2. _____ house

3. _____ for

4. _____ too

5. _____ singing

6. _____ certainly

7. _____ in

8. _____ underneath

9. _____ a

10. _____ below

11. _____ lightly

12. _____ however

13. _____ beyond

14. _____ occasionally

15. _____ inside

16. _____ crying

17. _____ speak

18. _____ upon

19. _____ outside

20. _____ bitterly

Prepositional Phrases

A preposition is always followed by a noun or pronoun called its **object**. Together, the preposition and its object form a **prepositional phrase**, as illustrated below.

Preposition	Object	Prepositional phrase
beyond	the stars	beyond the stars
inside	the NFL	inside the NFL
except for	them	except for them
with	his help	with his help
into	the room	into the room

> ### PRACTICING 2

Underline the prepositional phrase in each sentence. Some sentences may contain more than one prepositional phrase.

Example: I would hate to fall <u>into the lake</u>.

1. Don't be in a hurry to go up the stairs.

2. The scissors are on the table right before your eyes.

3. Because of his drinking, he lost the job.

4. She's sitting in the first row between JoRay and Harriett.

5. Bob left for school at 9:00 A.M.

6. A large part of his salary is used for rent.

7. The burglar hid behind the door in the attic.

8. Put glass in this recycling bin and paper in that one.

9. Margie stood in the cold and yelled, "Hello!"

10. We immediately headed down the street and through the alley.

Frequently Misused Prepositions

Although your speaker's ear is a fairly accurate guide to using prepositions, your ear may mislead you occasionally because of slang and the general informality of talk. Here are some frequently misused prepositions.

- **beside, besides.** *Beside* means *next to*, whereas *besides* means *in addition*.

  The comb is beside the brush.

  Besides planning the trip, she is also getting the tickets.

- **between, among.** Generally, *between* is used when two items are involved; with three or more, *among* is preferred.

  Between you and me, he is among friends.

- **due to.** *Due to* should not be used as a preposition meaning *because of*.

  Because of (not due to) his speeding, we were all ticketed.

- **inside of.** The *of* is always unnecessary.

  Stay inside the house.

  The man stayed outside (not *outside of*) the post office.

  Take your foot off (not *off of*) the table.

- **regarding, with respect to, in regard to.** Each of these three expressions sounds pompous. Use *about*.

    I want to speak to you about (not *regarding, with respect to,* or *in regard to*) your essay.

- **through, throughout.** *Through* means *by way of; throughout* means *in every part.*

    You drive through Bog Walk to get to Linstead.

    People are the same throughout the world.

- **toward, towards.** Both expressions are fine.

    He walked toward (towards) me.

PRACTICING 3

In the blank provided, write *C* if the preposition is used correctly and *NC* if it is not correct.

1. _____ Slowly, slowly, the bear moved towards the cabin.

2. _____ We have remained best friends throughout a decade.

3. _____ Once we found ourselves inside of the car, we felt safe.

4. _____ I am writing this letter in regard to your vacation.

5. _____ Because he was short, he decided not to play basketball.

6. _____ The money was divided between Marge, Alice, and Bob.

7. _____ She loves expensive things, and beside, she is abrasive.

8. _____ When you turn off Highway 5, go two miles.

9. _____ Get off of my property!

10. _____ Besides the weather being bad, the trip is too long.

Frequently Misused Expressions

The following expressions with prepositions are also frequently misused.

- **agree on, agree to.** *Agree on* is to be of one opinion, whereas *agree to* requires an action.

  They agreed on the terms of the contract.

  They agreed to get a divorce.

- **angry about, angry at, angry with.** *Angry about* is used for feeling of anger about a situation or condition, and *angry at* is used for anger directed at something specific, and *angry with* is used with people.

  Everyone was angry about being poor.

  We were angry at the weather.

  If you are angry with Sue, tell her so.

- **compare to, compare with.** *Compare to* shows similarities; *compare with* is not acceptable usage.

  Sons are often compared to their fathers.

- **differ with, differ from.** *Differ with* means to disagree, whereas *differ from* is to be unlike or dissimilar.

  I differ with you on the death penalty.

  Houses in Boston differ from the ones in San Francisco.

- **different than, different from.** *Different than* is not acceptable usage; always use *different from*.

  Annie is different from Joanie.

- **grateful to, grateful for.** You are *grateful to* a person, but *grateful for* something.

  We are grateful to Mrs. Smith.

  We are grateful for the sunshine.

- **independent of, independent from.** *Independent of* is the preferred usage.

  He is independent of any political party.

In a Nutshell

- A preposition shows the relationship between two things.

- Look out for some commonly misused expressions involving prepositions.

PRACTICING 4

In each pair of sentences, check the preferred version in the blank provided.

1. _____ **a.** Morrison was always independent of other rock bands.

   _____ **b.** Morrison was always independent from other rock banks.

2. _____ **a.** Joey differs from his father on the subject of taxes.

   _____ **b.** Joey differs with his father on the subject of taxes.

3. _____ **a.** Why should I be grateful to my good health?

   _____ **b.** Why should I be grateful for my good health?

4. _____ **a.** Indeed, we agreed to keeping the doors open.

   _____ **b.** Indeed, we agreed on keeping the doors open.

5. _____ **a.** I was shocked at how angry he was with me.

   _____ **b.** I was shocked at how angry he was about me.

6. _____ **a.** People can differ from each other on how to vote.

   _____ **b.** People can differ with each other on how to vote.

PRACTICING 5

Cross out the incorrect preposition in each sentence.

Example: My dreams differ (~~with,~~ from) my hopes.

1. My brother acts (like, as if) he's king of our house.

2. I am very envious (for, of) my rich cousin.

3. To be independent (of, from) my mother, I took a part-time job.

4. I am grateful (for, to) my student loan.

5. The dog died (of, with) old age.

6. We must all learn to comply (with, to) regulations.

7. My style of dressing contrasts (with, to) my sister's.

8. They agreed (on, to) the wedding date.

9. We were angry (about, at, with) having to face a war.

10. My brother differs (from, with) my father in looks.

UNIT TEST

In the blank provided, mark *C* if the italicized preposition or prepositional phrase is used correctly. Mark *NC* if it is not correct or not the best choice.

1. _____ Lay the book *besides* the flowers.

2. _____ Can't we agree *to* a single issue?

3. _____ Why is he so angry *with* his grandfather?

4. _____ Let's share the rent *between* us four buddies.

5. _____ Tell your dog to get *off of* my lawn right now!

6. _____ The dean wants to see Mike *in regard to* his grades.

7. _____ All children must some day become *independent from* their parents.

8. _____ Senator Smith *differs with* Senator Brown on how to pay for child care.

9. _____ I worked *throughout* the semester to learn more about astronomy.

10. _____ *Due to* her red hair she was called "Red Beauty."

UNIT TALKING ASSIGNMENT

A. Form a group. Use the following sentence as your topic. Write nine sentences supporting the topic, using prepositions in each one.

Computers exert a growing influence on our lives.

1. _____

_____

2. _____

_____

3. _____

_____

4. _____

_____

5. _____

_____

6. _____

_____

7. _____

_____

8. _____

_____

9. _____

_____

B. Now go back over the sentences and underline the prepositional phrases in each one.

UNIT WRITING ASSIGNMENT

Write about the influence of computers on our lives. Use ideas from the Unit Talking Assignment above and new ideas of your own.

Punctuation You Can Hear

"Charlie, will you please close the door?"

Punctuation marks are the traffic signs of writing. They tell the reader when to slow down, when to speed up, and when to stop. In writing, punctuation marks direct the eye's movement across the page. In spoken sentences, punctuation is heard as pauses, upbeats, and downbeats.

Ear Alert

Indeed, you can definitely hear some punctuation marks. For example, say the following sentences out loud:

> You are going home.

> You are going home?

> You are going home!

If you listen carefully to yourself, you will notice that you ended the first sentence on a pause, the second on an upbeat, and the third on a downbeat. These spoken cues help us tell the difference between a statement, a question, and a command.

In this unit we will discuss punctuation marks you can hear. These marks include end punctuation (periods, question marks, exclamation points), commas, and apostrophes. You can trust your speaker's ear to help you use these punctuation marks correctly.

End Punctuation

All sentences end with a period, a question mark, or an exclamation point. There are no exceptions to this rule.

Period (.)

Use a period after a sentence that makes a statement:

> My mother lost her wallet.

> Her car is in the garage.

Question mark (?)

Use a question mark after direct questions.

> Where did the sunshine go?

> Have you seen my pen?

The question mark is not used after an indirect question:

Mary asked where the sunshine had gone.

John wondered if we had seen his pen.

Exclamation point (!)

Use an exclamation point to show intense emotion, such as happiness, surprise, anger, or disgust, or to give a strong command:

What a fabulous day!

Get out of my house!

In a Nutshell

- Use a period at the end of a statement or indirect question.

- Use a question mark with direct questions.

- Use an exclamation point to indicate strong emotion or give a command.

PRACTICING 1

Place the proper punctuation mark at the end of each sentence.

Example: What would you do without me?

1. Is long hair attractive to women

2. I was very happy to hear about his grades

3. Save the whales

4. Is she as calm as she seems

5. They asked if we would be at home

6. Watch out

7. We waited in line for forty minutes

8. Are you driving or flying

9. Using your imagination, describe your ideal vacation

10. What an incredible bargain

The Comma (,)

You hear the comma as a half-pause. Sometimes the comma just makes listening or reading easier, but sometimes it is crucial to meaning. Here is an example:

Trying to escape, Alexander Gordon ran out the door.

Trying to escape Alexander, Gordon ran out the door.

The huge difference in the meanings of these two sentences depends on where the comma is placed. In the first sentence, *Alexander Gordon* is trying to escape an unknown someone or something. In the second, *Gordon* is trying to escape *Alexander*.

We will cover the hard and fast rules of comma usage.

Place a comma in front of coordinating conjunctions (and, but, or, for, nor, so, yet) that link independent clauses (see pp. 26–28).

He dodged the cold germs, but he caught pneumonia.

My mother is an accountant, and my father is her assistant.

He spoke with authority, so I believed him.

Do not use a comma before *and* if it is not followed by an independent clause.

Incorrect: He did the laundry, and made dinner.
Correct: He did the laundry and made dinner.

PRACTICING 2

Finish the following sentences by adding another independent clause and a coordinating conjunction. Remember to use a comma.

Example: The house she lived in was small <u>but it was wonderfully cozy.</u>

1. Be kind to all animals _____

2. I drive by that house daily _____

3. On Christmas we always stay home _____

4. I sat in the barber's chair _____

5. I believe people exist on other planets _____

6. Mother baked bread every Tuesday _____

7. The book was filled with pictures _____

8. Most repair people are honest _____

9. The embers glowed in the fireplace _____

10. She will probably break down and cry _____

Use a comma after introductory words, phrases, and clauses.

Words: Furthermore, he received a big bonus.

Well, why don't you move out?

Louise, I did it.

Phrases: From the point of view of health, he was perfect.

Having lost all, I really did not care what happened.

By the way, your mother called.

Clauses: Because it was raining, we stayed home.

but

We stayed home because it was raining.

(Use a comma after a dependent clause only if it comes at the beginning, but not at the end, of a sentence; see pp. 28–29.)

If I win the lottery, I will buy you the car.

but

I will buy you the car if I win the lottery.

In a Nutshell

Use commas after introductory words, phrases, and dependent clauses at the beginning of a sentence.

PRACTICING 3

Insert commas where needed.

1. Yes they can use the camping site.

2. As far as I am concerned everyone is invited.

3. Though feeling awkward John continued to dance.

4. Okay I'll work Saturday.

5. Elizabeth when are you leaving?

6. Moreover you owe me an apology for being late.

7. From behind the curtain he could not see his brother.

8. When you study the history of Russia you can understand why the farmers rebelled.

9. First of all none of us knows the future.

10. Scoring fifteen points he led the team.

PRACTICING 4

Insert commas where needed. In the space provided, state the rule that makes the comma necessary.

Correction: Mike, we were truly disappointed in your performance.

Rule: _A comma follows an introductory word._ _____

1. When students succeed in their studies they bring joy to their teachers.

Rule: _____

2. From the street we could see the flag at half mast.

Rule: _____

3. We went to the movies and then we stopped for coffee.

Rule: _____

4. If they had given us the right directions we would not have gotten lost.

Rule: _____

5. Furthermore he had no right to open her mail.

Rule: _____

6. Well why did you lend him the money if you knew he wouldn't repay you?

Rule: _____

7. Yes she is my cousin. No she does not speak English.

Rule: _____

8. He makes a good salary yet he doesn't have any savings.

Rule: _____

9. Are you stopping at the mall or are you going straight home?

Rule: _____

10. While we were watching the waves come in we saw a whale.

Rule: _____

Use commas to separate items in a series.

We ate steak, baked potatoes, and sweet corn.

The thick, juicy steak hit the spot.

You can read a book, watch television, or go to bed.

Up the road, through the woods, and along the river they trudged.

Do not, however, use commas unnecessarily with words in a series.

Do not use a comma before "and" if only two items are mentioned.

Incorrect: He plays the piano, and the trumpet.
Correct: He plays the piano and the trumpet.

Do not use a comma between modifiers unless you can insert the word "and" between them.

Incorrect: The old, red rowboat finally sank.
Correct: The old red rowboat finally sank.

You wouldn't say *The old and red rowboat finally sank*, so you shouldn't use a comma.

You would, however, use a comma between the modifiers of this sentence:

A cold, bitter wind blew off the lake.

You could insert the word *and* between the modifiers, and the sentence would still sound right.

A cold and bitter wind blew off the lake.

Do not use a comma before the first item in a series or after the last.

Incorrect: Other reasons to not smoke include, the smell, the expense, and the inconvenience.
Correct: Other reasons to not smoke include the smell, the expense, and the inconvenience.

Incorrect: You can add chocolate chips, raisins, or nuts, to the cookie batter.

Correct: You can add chocolate chips, raisins, or nuts to the cookie batter.

PRACTICING 5

Insert commas as necessary to separate items in a series.

1. They complain morning noon and night.

2. Give me some rollers a hairbrush and a blow dryer so I can make her look stylish.

3. I will climb the highest mountain swim the deepest ocean and struggle through the darkest jungle for a raise.

4. I need a hammer a saw and some nails.

5. The punch has Seven Up lemonade and sliced oranges in it.

6. Not everyone thought the dinner was tasty well priced and nutritious.

7. Pick one from column A one from column B and one from column C.

8. Would you like potatoes rice or beans?

9. The professor entered the room piled his books on the desk and began to hand out our papers.

10. I never watch anything on television except the news the movie reviews and the weather.

PRACTICING 6

In the following sentences, strike through the unnecessary commas.

Example: The elderly gentleman took off his hat, and sat down.

1. All of us need love, challenging work, and a sense of purpose, to be happy.

2. Give me some loyal, and amusing friends.

3. The kinds of textbooks I can't stand include, economics, finance, and math.

4. My first, real bicycle still sits in the attic.

5. Go ahead and serve the hors d'oeuvres, the salad, and the lemonade, before the guest of honor arrives.

6. Don't you enjoy listening to Elvis Presley, and the Beatles?

7. Other factors that make for pleasant camping include, smooth ground, leafy trees, and a running stream.

8. The old, Ford convertible was demolished.

9. My whole family plays tennis, and basketball.

10. For the picnic, we need, paper plates, napkins, and ants.

Place commas around words that interrupt the flow of a sentence.

In speaking, it is natural to pause before and after words that interrupt the flow of thought. In writing, this pause is signaled by a comma. Interruptions include the following:

Expression:	You must know by now, of course, that she is a very thoughtful person.
Descriptive phrase:	We struggled, cold and wet, to climb the mountain.
Prepositional phrase:	The dining room, into which we slowly trooped, was beautifully decorated.
Unessential clauses that begin with who, whose, which, when, where, or that:	The report, which took two weeks to write, earned Max a promotion.

A clause containing information that is not essential to understanding a sentence is enclosed by commas:

Mr. Jones, who wore a striped suit, caught a fly ball at the baseball game.	**(Because *Mr. Jones* is named, the information in the clause is not essential to identify him as the man who caught the ball.)**

On the other hand, the clause containing information essential to understanding the sentence is not punctuated by commas.

The man who wore the striped suit got hit by a baseball.

(Now the information in the clause is essential to identify who got hit by the baseball—the man in the striped suit, not the man in the gray suit.)

Commas needed: They repeatedly played *One Love*, which is a song I'd never heard before.

Commas not needed: They repeatedly played a song that I'd never heard before.

Most of the time, relative clauses with *which* need commas, whereas relative clauses with *that* do not.

Commas needed: The sloop *Spray II*, which I usually sail, is tied up at the dock.

Commas not needed: The sloop that I usually sail is tied up at the dock.

In a Nutshell

- Use commas to set off expressions and phrases that interrupt a sentence.

- Use commas to set off clauses that contain information not essential to understanding the sentence.

PRACTICING 7

Use commas to set off the unessential interruptions in these sentences. If the sentence is correct, leave it alone.

Example: My uncle Albert**,** who is my favorite relative**,** is here tonight.

1. Mr. Clark who shouted over the microphone as loudly as possible could not be heard.

2. Our coach whom we really admire won the Best Teacher Award.

3. The incision which left a large scar needed plastic surgery.

4. Any official who takes a bribe should be ashamed.

5. The sky covered with billowy white clouds made me want to write a poem.

6. We went to hear the astronaut who had walked on the moon.

7. My uncle who had served in two major wars still had his uniforms.

8. The old family home where my brother now lives needs remodeling.

9. My neighbor who teaches first grade is very friendly.

10. Give this ticket to the man who is standing at the gate and to no one else.

PRACTICING 8

Underline the words that interrupt the flow of the sentence, then place commas around them.

Example: My brother, <u>who always hated suits</u>, wants a tuxedo for his birthday.

1. His father loved and respected by all members of the family just turned 85.

2. Her wedding expected for so many years took place last month.

3. Peter Dunkin who is very graceful and coordinated will be the lead dancer.

4. Our English teacher a fanatic about spelling won the spelling bee in elementary school.

5. Old people often neglected by their families need community help to remain independent.

6. All the children in our neighborhood considered Harry the local bakery owner a great hero.

7. Dr. Jensen who gave the commencement address kept his audience entertained.

8. Identity as a worker especially for males is a psychological necessity.

9. All cultures you realize are becoming more and more technological.

10. She is by the way my aunt.

Use commas for dates and addresses and in the openings and closings of letters.

Commas to separate items of a date:	My twentieth birthday party took place on Tuesday, March 14, 1996.
	By July 9, 1997, the whole balance on the car will be due.
Commas to separate items of an address:	Alicia lives at 30 Munson Drive, Detroit, Michigan, 40202.
	Mail the card to 1500 North Verdugo Road, Glendale, California, 34525.
Commas in the openings and closings of letters and in numbers:	Dearest Caroline, Dear Juan, Yours truly, Sincerely,

In a Nutshell

Use commas for dates and addresses and in the openings and closings of letters.

PRACTICING 9

Insert commas in the following sentences. Some sentences may require no commas.

1. On Monday September 4 we celebrated Labor Day.

2. My dear Mrs. Wong

3. We will stay at the campgrounds from Monday August 27 to Friday September 1.

4. We moved from Huntington Beach to La Mirada.

5. Pasquale's hair salon has moved to 420 Camden Drive.

6. Dear Teddy

7. Sincerely yours

8. They used to live at 6201 Main Street.

9. Dear Mary

10. Now she lives at 2322 Chevy Chase Drive Lansing Michigan.

11. I will be gone from Friday March 10 1995 until Monday January 1 1996.

12. Send Peter's mail to 933 Andover Street Worthington Ohio 43085.

13. We drove from Jackson Hole to Aspen.

14. Mary was born August 12 1978 and Kevin was born on February 5 1983.

15. Is she from Miami Ohio or Miami Florida?

Use commas to set off direct quotations from the rest of the sentence.

A quotation may be either direct—exactly what someone said—or indirect—a report of what someone said.

Direct
Quotation: "Forget you ever saw me," he whispered.

Indirect
Quotation: He said to forget she had ever seen him.

Direct quotations can be reported in three ways, each requiring commas.

"Forget you ever saw me," he whispered.

"Forget," he whispered, "you ever saw me."

He whispered, "Forget you ever saw me."

Commas and periods always go inside the quotation marks (see pp. 214–215).

PRACTICING 10

Add commas to set off the quoted material from the rest of the sentence.

1. "Steve has a new job" he announced.

2. "The results" he insisted "speak for themselves."

3. "I have never drunk anything stronger than Coca Cola" he replied.

4. Frederico insisted "It's a perfect day for the picnic."

5. The clerk said "Shoes and shirts are required."

6. "I ordered one deluxe pizza" she answered.

7. "I certainly didn't mean any harm" indicated Barry "but I had to tell the truth."

8. "Let's go downstairs and do the laundry" Linda suggested.

9. "Stacking the books on the shelf" he told Rhonda "is very time-consuming."

10. "They do not resemble each other one bit" he noted.

The Apostrophe (')

The apostrophe has two uses, to show possession and to indicate a contraction.

Use the apostrophe to show possession.

The chart below shows how apostrophes are used to show possession or ownership. For a singular noun, always add 's. However, to form the possessive of a plural noun ending in s, add only the apostrophe. If the plural does not end in s, add 's.

Singular (always add 's)	Plural
girl's notebook	girls' notebooks
bus's driver	buses' drivers
child's toy	children's toys
Carl Keith's house	the Keiths' house

PRACTICING 11

Make the following nouns possessive. First decide if the noun is singular or plural. Then decide if you need only an apostrophe or 's.

1. the Smiths lawn

2. the lion mane

3. the firefighters trucks

4. the grass color

5. the men hats

6. the bus horn

7. the churches bells

8. the tulips petals

9. the police officers promotions

10. the years memories

Use the apostrophe to show an omission in a contraction.

Apostrophes are used to show omitted letters in contractions, such as *don't* (do not) or *isn't* (is not). Contractions are commonly used in informal writing. Here are some common contractions:

can not	can't
could have	could've
could not	couldn't
did not	didn't
do not	don't
has not	hasn't
have not	haven't
he is	he's
I am	I'm
I would	I'd
it is	it's
she is	she's
should have	should've
should not	shouldn't
they are	they're
they are not	they aren't
who is	who's
will not	won't
would have	would've
would not	wouldn't
let us	let's

Ear Alert

In speech, we can hear these contractions. What we cannot hear is exactly where the apostrophe goes—where the letter was actually omitted.

couldn't, not could'nt   **(the apostrophe marks the omission of the <u>o</u>)**

they're, not theyr'e   **(the apostrophe marks the omission of the <u>a</u>)**

Remember to put the apostrophe exactly where the letter is missing.

Do not use apostrophes unnecessarily.

Only use an apostrophe with a possessive.

> **Incorrect:**   Apple's are on sale this week.
>
> **Correct:**   Apples are on sale this week.

To test whether a noun is possessive or not, turn it into an *of* phrase.

The book's cover is red.	**(book's cover = cover of the book = possessive)**
The library books' are due.	**(books' are = the are of the book = not possessive)**

Do not use apostrophes with the pronouns *his, hers, its, ours, yours,* or *theirs*.

> **Incorrect:**   The sweater is hers'.
>
> **Correct:**   The sweater is hers.

> **Incorrect:**   The cat washed it's face.
>
> **Correct:**   The cat washed its face.

It's is a contraction—short for *it is*. If you unravel the contraction, you get

> The cat washed it is face.

which makes no sense.

In a Nutshell

- Use the apostrophe to show possession.

- Use the apostrophe to mark omitted letters in a contraction.

- Do not use unnecessary apostrophes.

PRACTICING 12

Rewrite the following sentences to use contractions whenever possible.

Example: We could not remember their names.

   We couldn't remember their names.

1. Why in the world would you not want to help out?

_____

2. We could not have studied harder.

_____

3. Ten years from now it will not matter in the least.

_____

4. They were not the least excited about being on television.

_____

5. If Manny had not eaten, he would have offended the hostess.

_____

6. Surely you could have been more tactful.

_____

7. Why are they not planning to meet us at the movie?

_____

8. If Felice had been polite, we would have included her.

_____

9. Of all the things you should not have said, that was the worst.

_____

10. Who is this funny man?

_____

PRACTICING 13

Insert apostrophes where needed.

1. Many peoples attitudes toward taxes have changed.

2. Theyre sick of having to clean up everyone elses mess.

3. Mothers worry is needless.

4. Who hasnt hung his coat on the rack?

5. Doesnt it matter to you that they believe you lied?

6. New Yorks tall buildings amaze foreigners.

7. The essays titles were most imaginative.

8. His fathers fishing rod was in the garage.

9. The companys morale was at an all-time low.

10. Jeffs uncle is a nice person.

PRACTICING 14

Turn the phrases below into possessives.

Example: the book of Jack.

Answer: Jack's book

1. the umbrella of Lucy

_____

2. the fence of the garden

_____

3. the gun of the warden

_____

4. the fur of the cat

_____

5. the seat of the driver

_____

6. the house of Mel

_____

7. the meager food of the people

_____

8. the cars of James

_____

9. the treatment of the doctor

_____

10. the complaint of most guests

_____

PRACTICING 15

Every sentence below has one apostrophe error. It may be missing an apostrophe (or *'s*) in a possessive or in a contraction. Sometimes the error is an unnecessary apostrophe. Add apostrophes (or *'s*) where they are needed. Strike out all unnecessary apostrophes.

1. You should add potatoes and bean's to the stew.

2. Werent you surprised to see Jenny's boyfriend

   there?

3. I think the red convertible is Johns.

4. The mountain bike is her's.

5. I get two weeks vacation this year.

6. That shirt is missing two button's.

7. Its not clear whether the party is at Jane's or Bill's

   house.

8. The job is your's if you want it.

9. Hanging by it's tail, the monkey chattered.

10. The volleyball players uniforms are purple and white.

UNIT TEST

In the blank provided, mark *C* if the sentence is correctly punctuated; mark *NC* if it is not correct.

Example: <u>NC</u> When did they leave town.

1. _____ What could you possibly want from me!

2. _____ She asked when the wedding would take place?

3. _____ We bought all kinds of green vegetables but they
        rotted.

4. _____ As a matter of fact you should do the dishes.

5. _____ Since you prefer carrot cake, I baked one for you.

6. _____ Birds fly, dogs bark, and bees buzz.

7. _____ Your need to bring, a flash light, a sleeping bag, and
        some dried food.

8. _____ She was however unable to follow the directions.

9. _____ John whose last name started with an "A" went first.

10. _____ We arrived, worn out but happy, at the summit of the mountain.

11. _____ Any mother, who loves her child, will be concerned with the child's diet.

12. _____ Dwight D. Eisenhower a general of World War II was also president of the United States.

13. _____ We graduated on Saturday, May 16 1996.

14. _____ The letter was sent to 926 Mayfair Lane, Columbus, Ohio.

15. _____ "Let's pledge allegiance to the flag, " he said.

16. _____ "None of this would have happened" he said "if you had swept the floor."

17. _____ That coat is not hers'; it's his.

18. _____ Its about time for you to grow up and quit whimpering.

19. _____ If you are'nt sure, don't volunteer the answer.

20. _____ Its the Millers' back yard.

UNIT TALKING ASSIGNMENT

A. Dictate the following sentences to a chosen partner using pauses, upbeats, and downbeats to indicate the necessary punctuation. The goal of this exercise is for your partner to insert the appropriate punctuation mainly by ear, based on your reading.

1. Call me again sometime you lovely man

2. Were you startled to see her

3. I took his advice and went to see her

4. Give me eggs potatoes and hamburger thats all I want.

5. He told his soldiers This is your time to achieve glory

6. This is what you must do Sit down take a breath and then give the answer

7. Did you really see an eagle

8. Mrs Gooch our student advisor said This should be our goal.

9. Lees car is a really sleek machine

10. Mr. Smiths dog which now weighs more than I do was happy to see us

B. Punctuate the following sentences, using the same approach as in exercise A, with your partner now doing the dictating.

1. Run for your life

2. What can you learn that will help you understand this neighborhood

3. Much to my pleasure some of my fathers money will go to my sister

4. Benjamin Franklin 1706 to 1790 made his fortune as a printer editor inventor and a statesman

5. When did you move to South Dakota

6. A mans home is his castle

7. Theyre so much alike

8. Although these statistics were questioned by experts they struck a chord with the average person.

9. Where are you going she asked and why cant I go with you

10. Shouldn't you be getting ready to leave

UNIT WRITING ASSIGNMENT

Write a paragraph about what your best friend means to you. Include a conversation that is typical of your relationship. Be specific and focus particularly on the rules of punctuation we have just covered.

Punctuation You Can't Hear

"I drank tea for breakfast; then I ate a muffin."

Your ear may often tell you when a pause means a comma or an upbeat means a question mark. At other times your ear is of little use in identifying the correct punctuation. For certain punctuation marks, you must simply learn the rules. In this unit you will learn how to use the punctuation marks we generally can't accurately hear:

■ the semicolon

■ the colon

■ the dash

■ quotation marks

■ parentheses

Semicolon (;)

The semicolon has a beat somewhere between a period and a comma— too fine for most of us to hear. It is a punctuation mark more commonly associated with writing than with speaking. In writing the semicolon has two main uses.

Use a semicolon to join two closely related, complete thoughts not connected by a conjunction, such as "and," "but," "or," "for," or "nor."

The winds were as high as 50 mph; tiles flew off our roof.

Bats were roosting in the attic; the renters still stayed.

Notice the close relationship between the thoughts expressed in both sentences. In the first sentence, the tiles flew off the roof because the winds were high. In the second, the renters stayed in spite of the bats. So closely related are these thoughts that both sentences could have been written with a coordinating conjunction.

The winds were as high as 50 mph, so tiles flew off our roof.

Bats were roosting in the attic, yet the renters stayed.

PRACTICING 1

Place a semicolon between the two breaks in thought in each of the following sentences.

1. I ate a muffin after I finished it I drank some orange juice.

2. A camel can go for weeks without water it stores water in its hump.

3. He sat listening to the conversation at the next table it made him chuckle.

4. Bertha had to leave the movie all the bloodshed made her sick.

5. I dislike shopping during the holidays people are so rude and in such a hurry.

Use a semicolon between two complete thoughts joined by the transitions "however," "thus," "therefore," "consequently," "moreover," "furthermore," "nevertheless," or "otherwise."

To finish the house, we have to work overtime; however, we may still not succeed.

She loved to go to the theater; moreover, she felt she had acting talent.

Note that a comma comes after the transition.

In a Nutshell

- Use a semicolon to connect two complete thoughts not separated by *and*, *but*, *or*, *for*, or *nor*.

- Use a semicolon between two sentences joined by the transitions *however*, *thus*, *therefore*, *consequently*, *moreover*, *furthermore*, *nevertheless*, or *otherwise*.

- Use a comma after the transition words.

PRACTICING 2

Choose an appropriate transition from the nutshell box on page 208 to complete the sentences below. Place a semicolon before the transition and a comma after it.

Example: He stopped by the house*;* _however,_ we had no food to offer him.

1. Annie was bogged down with homework _____ her mother typed her term paper for her.

2. He was told to turn left at the gas station _____ he turned right.

3. He received a grant _____ he worked cutting people's lawns.

4. He had to get some rest _____ he might have failed the exam.

5. They could find only red balloons _____ they changed the theme to "loving hearts."

PRACTICING 3

Place semicolons where needed. Use commas after transitional words.

1. Poverty means being tired moreover, it means being tired day after day.

2. Yesterday my battery went dead consequently I am walking to work today.

3. Educated people tend to be open-minded and curious uneducated people tend to be closed-minded and set in their ways.

4. American families are dominated by television it stunts our minds.

5. I like her a lot however I love you.

6. Betty loves her neighborhood nevertheless she wishes it were more safe.

7. People who walk two miles every day feel better they can also eat a dessert now and then.

8. Stand tall be proud.

9. Large, leafy trees provide shade they also need much water.

10. He was utterly generous he gave money to everyone in town.

Colon (:)

The colon is used to introduce something that follows—a list, a quotation, or further explanation:

List: These are the people who will sit at the head table: the mayor, all City Council members, the trustees of the College, and the master of ceremonies.

Quotation: This is what S. J. Lee had to say about heaven: "What a pity that the only way to heaven is in a hearse!"

Further explanation: When police violate the law, they encourage contempt for the law: People simply will not obey laws that the people in authority do not obey.

If the material after the colon is a complete sentence, begin with a capital letter.

In a Nutshell

- Use a colon to introduce material that follows, such as a list, a quotation, or a further explanation.

- If the material after the colon is a complete sentence, begin with a capital letter.

PRACTICING 4

Add colons where they belong. Capitalize after the colon if necessary.

1. This is what John. F. Kennedy said about poverty "if a free society cannot help the many who are poor, it cannot save the few who are rich."

2. Here is the author's name David Halberstam.

3. Today's typical home office contains several necessary machines a computer, a duplicator, a fax , and a message service.

4. There is one positive result from having a migraine headache the next day you feel better than ever.

5. There is one thing stronger than all the armies in the world it is an idea whose time has come.

The Dash (--)

The dash—is often typed as two hyphens (--). It is spoken as a short pause, like a comma. A dash is used in writing to signal a sudden break in thought or to emphasize a side comment or an afterthought. Here are some examples:

Sudden break in thought:	He would like to be polite—just as all of us would like to be.
	I spoke at length to the audience—at least, it seemed long to me.
Side thought:	Democracy is based on sharing the good things in life—especially power.
	I would hate myself—and so should all children who have had good mothers— if I neglected my mother now that she is old.
Afterthought:	I became interested in bird watching, gardening, and oil painting—all hobbies I had never had before.
	If you want to be imaginative, you have to be willing to tolerate criticism—even ridicule.

Don't overuse the dash, or your style will seem breathless.

In a Nutshell

- Use the dash to emphasize a sudden break in thought or to add a side comment or afterthought.

- Do not overuse the dash.

> **PRACTICING 5**

Use dashes to set off sudden breaks in thought, side thoughts, and afterthoughts in the sentences below.

1. You owe me $10.00 oh, I'm sorry I thought you were someone else.

2. I asked her I begged her to pays the bills on time.

3. Do you blame others especially society for the way your marriage has turned out?

4. I need a new computer or at least a few more chips for memory.

5. She's not my real mother not that that makes any difference.

Quotation Marks (" ")

One of the two main written uses for quotations marks is to indicate a person's exact words—called a direct quotation.

Use quotation marks to indicate a person's exact words.

Direct quotations can be reported in a number of different ways, all requiring quotation marks.

> She said, "You know I love you."

> "You know I love you," she said.

> "You know," she said, "I love you."

> "You know I love you," she said. "I miss you."

Begin every quotation with a capital letter.
Do not, however, use a capital letter for the second part of a divided quotation that is *not* a full sentence.

> "I became a librarian," he explained, "because I love books."

Here the second part of the divided quotation is not a full sentence, so a comma is used after *explained*, but no capital letter.

> "Put the book on the table," the librarian said. "I'll shelve it later."

Here the second part of the divided quotation is a full sentence. A period and a capital letter follow *said*.

Do not use quotation marks in indirect quotations.
An indirect quotation—rewording what someone has said—does not require quotation marks. Often an indirect quotation word is announced by the word *that*. Here are some examples:

Direct quotation:	Jane said, "Dad will be down in ten minutes."
Indirect quotation:	Jane told us that Dad will be down in ten minutes.
Direct quotation:	His card said, "I love you beyond measure."
Indirect quotation:	His card said that he loved her beyond measure.

In a Nutshell

- Use quotation marks to indicate a person's exact words.

- Begin every quotation with a capital letter.

- Do not use a capital letter for the second part of a divided quotation that is not a sentence.

- Do not use quotation marks in indirect quotations.

PRACTICING 6

Add the required quotation marks.

Example: "I'm calling you," said the salesman, "because you filled out our form."

1. Try to look at it my way, through the corner of your eye, said Audrey.

2. You know I love ice cream, said David. Chocolate is my favorite.

3. When have I ever asked you to make dinner? she asked.

4. Watch out, she murmured. I'm going to tickle you.

5. Jenny asked, Has the mailman arrived yet?

6. You can't remember the sermon, interrupted Mr. Smith, because you were not in church when it was delivered.

7. It's not a bad feeling to be kissed, the teenager laughed; it's actually a good feeling.

8. Letting his arms droop, he answered, Oh, I'm just tired.

9. If I don't get to have a bath soon, Agnes declared, I'll start itching all over.

10. He said, I like coming here because the place makes me happy.

PRACTICING 7

Place quotation marks only around the exact words of the speaker; leave the sentence unchanged if the quotation is indirect.

1. We asked ourselves, How long will they be gone?

2. Rachel asked him if he would return before sunset.

3. Aaron asked his mother if her boss had been rude again.

4. Marge promised that she would make a special effort.

5. Tell us about the accident, we said.

Using other punctuation with quotation marks

- Commas and periods always go inside quotation marks.
  He said, "I am not going."
  He said, "I am not going," and then added, "at least, not today."

- Question marks and exclamation points go either inside or outside, depending on the sentence.

  Inside: "Is he just making a wild guess?" Larry asked.

  Outside: Who just said, "He's making a wild guess"?

In the first example, the spoken words make up a separate question; in the second example, the spoken words are part of the question.

"Watch out!" Karen cried.

Karen, stop saying, "Watch out"!

In the first example, the spoken words make up a separate command; in the second, the spoken words are part of the command.

In a Nutshell

- Always put periods and commas inside quotation marks.

- Question marks and exclamation points go either inside or outside quotation marks, depending on the sentence.

PRACTICING 8

The sentences that follow use other punctuation marks in connection with quotation marks. In the space provided, mark *C* if the sentence is correctly punctuated and *NC* if it is not. Correct the sentence if it is incorrectly punctuated.

Example: ___C___ "Are you happy?" she asked.

1. _____ The teacher said to Leo, "Explain your answer."

2. _____ Was it Snoopy who asked, "Do you like dogs"?

3. _____ She screamed, "I love that story"!

4. _____ Who said, "I think; therefore, I am?"

5. _____ "Get off my lawn!" she screamed.

6. _____ What is the meaning of "Blessed are the poor"?

7. _____ Stop telling me to "shut up!"

8. _____ She loudly cried, "Give me some air, please!"

9. _____ "No, never!" she insisted.

10. _____ He asked, "Have you actually read that book?"

Use quotation marks to indicate titles of short works.

Use quotation marks to indicate the titles of short works, such as magazine articles and short stories. Underline (or italicize) the titles of long works.

Shorter works	**Longer works**
magazine article—"Easy Desserts"	magazine—<u>Healthy Eating</u>
newspaper article—"Life Begins at 50"	newspaper—<u>The Atlanta Journal</u>
song—"My Achey Breaky Heart"	book—<u>David Copperfield</u>
poem—"Mary Had a Little Lamb"	poetry collection—<u>Leaves of Grass</u>
book chapter—"The Darkness Appears"	movie—<u>12 Monkeys</u>
editorial—"The Crash of Flight 592"	television series—<u>Friends</u>

In a Nutshell

- Use quotation marks to indicate the titles of short works.
- Underline (or italicize) the titles of longer works.

PRACTICING 9

Add quotation marks or underline as required.

Example: "A Delicate Operation" is an essay that appears in an anthology titled <u>Subject and Strategy</u>.

1. Chapter 1 is titled Mattie Michael.

2. My sister was going to read the book The Littlest Angel.

3. The Prince of Tides is a good movie.

4. One of my favorite songs is Gimme Shelter by the Rolling Stones.

5. She searched through the book Great Italian Recipes.

6. People magazine is filled with juicy gossip.

7. The San Francisco Chronicle is a fine newspaper.

8. As a movie The Piano did not appeal to me because it was so unrealistic.

9. The Taming of the Shrew is my favorite Shakespeare play.

10. My wife likes to watch the television series Seinfeld.

Parentheses ( )

Use parentheses for side comments that illustrate a point or add information. They are also used to enclose numbers when you list items.

To illustrate a point:	Curiosity (the kind exemplified by Edison and Newton) is one mark of intelligence.
	My brother and his friend (the best man at his wedding, actually) were both rushed to the emergency ward.

To add information:	The Ritz-Carlton hotels train their managers in Total Quality Management (TQM).
	The average person (the so-called "reasonable man") used to be defined as male by the English language.
	Brad Anderson (b. 1924) is my favorite cartoonist.
	The author explains precisely how the team works (see p. 53). **(Place the period *after* the parentheses in references.)**
With numbers:	Here are the rules: (1) Keep your room clean, (2) be on time, and (3) don't complain about the food.

In a Nutshell

- Use parentheses to add an illustration or side remark to a sentence.

- Use parentheses with numbers.

PRACTICING 10

Add parentheses where needed.

1. Edward M. Kennedy b. 1932 is the younger brother of President John F. Kennedy.

2. The chapter on civil rights pages 85–98 covers the attitudes of the white moderates.

3. The chapter on moving westward pp. 25–36 will be on the test.

4. It was freezing weather 13 degrees Fahrenheit.

5. The National Endowment for the Arts NEA may have its budget severely slashed.

UNIT TEST

Each sentence in the following passage contains a punctuation error. Correct it.

Russell Baker 1925–present began his career in journalism in 1947 as a staff member of the *Baltimore Sun*. Today, his newspaper articles have been collected in book form for two reasons they are simple and they reveal life as many of us have experienced it. The other day, I asked my classmate Deanna, Do you ever read Russell Baker? She answered, Of course not. I hate reading in my spare time. I pointed out to her that she would enjoy Baker's essay entitled Meaningful Relationships. I said, It discusses the modern approach to love. Are you crazy? she asked me. Why would I waste my time reading about love when I can see a movie about love? Look, I replied, Reading is good for you. I left the room thinking to myself, What a superficial person you are. You probably don't even read The Baltimore Sun, your local newspaper.

UNIT TALKING ASSIGNMENT

A. Choose a partner to whom you dictate the following sentences. See if your partner can write them down with the correct punctuation.

1. "Whose book is this?" she asked Tom.
2. Ten years ago we heard, "Learn word processing." Now we hear, "Get on the Internet."
3. "You backed into my car!" she cried.
4. Was it Franco who asked, "May I borrow a dollar"?
5. The title of the poem is, "How Tall Is the Mountain?"

B. Reversing the process, have your partner dictate the following sentences to you. Write them down with correct punctuation.

1. Mother warned, "It's raining cats and dogs."
2. We knew who he meant when he said, "She's gone."
3. "He won! He won! He won!" we chanted in unison.
4. "What is her real name?" he muttered to himself.
5. Who said, "Give me liberty or give me death"?

UNIT WRITING ASSIGNMENT

Imagine that you are disturbed about a critical remark someone made about your best friend. Recreate the incident, and include an imaginary conversation between you and your friend's critic. The point is to punctuate correctly. Be especially careful to use quotation marks where they belong.

Index

NOTES

NOTES

NOTES

NOTES

NOTES

NOTES